THE OBEDIENCE OF FAITH

STUDIES IN BIBLICAL THEOLOGY

A series of monographs designed to provide clergy and laymen with the best
work in biblical scholarship both in this country and abroad

STUDIES IN BIBLICAL THEOLOGY

Second Series · 19

THE OBEDIENCE OF FAITH

*The Purposes of Paul in the Epistle
to the Romans*

PAUL S. MINEAR

SCM PRESS LTD
BLOOMSBURY STREET LONDON

334 01146 9
FIRST PUBLISHED 1971
© SCM PRESS LTD 1971
PRINTED IN GREAT BRITAIN BY
W & J MACKAY & CO LTD, CHATHAM

To Grace Frick and
Marguerite Yourcenar

Paul S. Minear is a Ph.D. of Yale University (1932) and an LL.D. of Iowa Wesleyan University (1942). From 1933–4 he was Assistant Professor, Hawaii School of Religion, Honolulu; Professor, Garrett Biblical Institute (1933–44); Norris Professor, Andover Newton Theological School (1944–56); Winkley Professor of Biblical Theology, Yale Divinity School (1959–70). In 1970 he was appointed Vice Rector, Ecumenical Institute for Advanced Theological Study, Jerusalem.

Dr Minear is the author of a number of books including: *An Introduction to Paul* (1937); *And Great Shall be Your Reward* (1941); *Eyes of Faith* (1946); *The Choice* (1948); *The Kingdom and the Power* (1950); *Christian Hope and the Second Coming* (1954); *Jesus and His People* (1956); *Images of the Church in the New Testament* (1960); *The Gospel according to Mark* (*Layman's Bible Commentaries*, 1962); and *I Saw a New Earth* (Corpus Books, 1969).

CONTENTS

PREFACE

It would be outright folly for me to try to match wits with the author of Romans. Attempts to cope with Paul's thought quickly force any reader far beyond his depth. In fact, unless he confesses that this goal exceeds his grasp, he has not even begun to grasp. One test of any commentary is the degree to which it conveys a sense of the range and deftness, the subtlety and complexity, of the apostle's mind. By this test, Karl Barth's commentary, with all its defects, remains the greatest Pauline study of our time.

It may not be such blatant folly, however, for me to cross swords with various modern commentators on the epistle. Unless I believed this, I would not have written this book. It is my view that in their studies of this epistle many scholars have chosen wrong options, followed wrong roads and have, as a consequence, rendered Paul's meaning less accessible than it should be. To these false turnings scholars have been led by faulty conceptions of the situation in Rome, of the resulting reactions of the apostle, and thus of the whole character of his letter. For example, in many treatments it has been the habit to assume that believers in Rome formed a single congregation. I think that, on the contrary, all the evidence points to the existence of several congregations, separated from each other by sharp mutual suspicions. It is customary to view the epistle as a treatise in systematic or dogmatic theology, moving from one doctrinal theme to another. I think it reflects a primary concern with pastoral problems and therefore presents a continuous argument designed to meet specific situations in Rome. Many readers suppose that the message is quite independent of the occasion; in principle the letter might have been sent anywhere without altering the ideas. I think Paul would have found such an attitude inconceivable. Again, it is customary to suppose that the most significant passages are to be found in the early chapters. Along with Willi Marxsen, I am convinced that 'the peculiar feature of this letter is that its main message comes at the end'. Because Paul's objectives are made clear at the end, the earlier paragraphs are oriented towards the realization of those objectives. Should readers discover that this approach enhances their understanding of the epistle, I shall be content.

Several debts should be acknowledged. First to that sturdy company of scholars who produced the Revised Standard Version of the Bible, the translation which I have adopted except where an alternative source is indicated. I thank students at Andover Newton Theological School and at Yale Divinity School, for without their encouraging response to lectures on this theme the project would never have been undertaken. Thanks also go to Yale University, since this study could not have been completed apart from a triennial semester on leave. The progress of the work has been accelerated by gracious hospitality extended by the Institute for Ecumenical and Cultural Research at St John's University. My wife has guarded the text against egregious blunders in style and substance. Mrs Helen R. Kent has reduced successive revisions to the legibility of typescript with amazing equanimity and expertness. To all these, sincere thanks.

PAUL S. MINEAR

I

THE PURPOSES IN OUTLINE: SITUATIONS REFLECTED IN 14.1–16.27

In these chapters our goal is a more adequate understanding of the occasion which induced Paul to send his epistle to the congregations in Rome. Our title suggests one formulation of that occasion and purpose. Having heard of certain urgent needs in those congregations, Paul wrote to them in order 'to bring about the obedience of faith' (1.5). We should take that assertion of his motivation with complete seriousness, as more than a perfunctory and pious cliché. Why? Because in his closing benediction, the apostle returned to this obedience as the goal of 'my gospel and the preaching of Jesus Christ' (16.25f.). Nor was he content with mentioning this goal at the beginning and end of his letter. He defined the two key factions within the churches as the strong versus the weak in faith, and on many points he indicated his concern with their common disobedience to faith (16.19). In fact, Paul asserted that the single comprehensive drive of his apostolic work had been 'to win obedience from the Gentiles' (15.18). The obedience of 'one man' had provided the pattern (5.19) according to which every believer's obedience was both demanded and tested (6.12–18). Such obedience, emerging from a strengthened faith, was the goal not only of the letter to Rome but of his anticipated trip there (1.11). We may conclude, then, that Paul saw the basic occasion for his letter as the need in the Roman churches for a stronger, more obedient faith. His intention was to contribute, in so far as he could, to meeting that need.

But this general statement needs elaboration. The phrase 'to bring about the obedience of faith' is theological shorthand for a subtle set of intentions which were prompted by the existence of a very tangled and tense set of circumstances. The writing of the letter was related to at least two things: (1) the immediate and the

long-term plans of the apostle at the time of writing, (2) the difficulties which had been reported *within the congregations in Rome*.

Because the information available on the first of these is so
definite, it is well to begin with Paul's own plans at the time of his
writing. He had long placed on his agenda a campaign to Spain.
For that trip it was necessary to travel through Rome, for obvious
geographical reasons as well as for less obvious logistic reasons
(1.8–15; 15.14–33). However, his projected trip had been frustrated time after time (1.13; 15.22). What the obstacles were is not
entirely clear. Paul's apostolic work in the east was a factor, for he
wished to finish the job there before going west. Probably also to
be reckoned with were the difficulties Paul was having with the
unruly factions in Corinth. It is probable that among those difficulties was the opposition among Gentile Christians to the collection of the fund for Jerusalem. At least the delivery of that fund
was the last item on the apostle's itinerary before his planned
departure for Rome (15.28). All the other reasons for delay had
now been removed – stimulus enough for writing to his future
hosts. But let us look more closely at two features in his itinerary.

1. The visit to Spain

There were logistic reasons for writing to the Romans in connection with that visit, although Paul is not very explicit about
them. Certainly this letter reminds us of Paul's penchant for planning his travels well in advance; he would go from Corinth, by
way of Ephesus, to Jerusalem, thence to Rome, and thence to
Spain. Between the lines we can read the traveller's desire for a
chance to rest in Rome ('to enjoy your company') and for shoring
up his financial resources ('to be sped on my journey there by
you'). More important, though less certain, we may suppose that
Paul wanted to avoid the catastrophe of having his work in Spain
ruined by opposition from the Roman congregations. He had
learned how important for missionary activity is a loyal base, a
city where various congregations share whole-heartedly in a
common enterprise. Nothing more quickly jeopardized the sur-
vival of infant churches than strife among supporting churches.
Paul was unable to forget what had happened in Antioch, Galatia,
Philippi and Corinth, where competing evangelists and prophets
had challenged his credentials and disrupted his work. Nor did the
rumours from Rome augur well for his plans. Among the Roman

saints tensions similar to those in Galatia and Philippi had prevented common worship and had denied a common witness. It was altogether probable that Paul would not receive the hospitality and support which he needed. Therefore the reconciliation of the Roman saints held top priority in his preparation for a mission to Spain. Thus a very simple fact – the plans to go to Spain – prompted a very obvious intention: the desire to secure full Roman support. And this intention evoked a strong concern for reconciling the antagonists among the Roman Christians.

2. The journey to Jerusalem

Before Rome, however, came Jerusalem. And this was more than a place on the map, more than a step towards a longer journey. This journey was a major goal of Paul's apostleship, in part because it represented the accomplishment of his pledge to the other apostles (Gal. 2.10), a pledge which he wanted to complete before going to Rome. Having collected a considerable sum from several Gentile churches he was under obligation to obtain its safe delivery to the 'poor saints' in Jerusalem. Financial drives are so routine in our modern churches that we readily overlook the strategic importance of that first drive. It was a startling innovation. Gentile Christians in Macedonia and Achaea had been asked to send money to poor Jewish Christians in Jerusalem. Earlier appeals had been resisted; Paul's authority had been rejected. There were rumours that the whole business was graft. Unaccustomed to almsgiving, having few resources of their own, despising the Jews, resenting the ways in which Jewish Christians had opposed the Gentile mission and churches, Paul's Gentile churches were brought to open rebellion on this issue. It seems that the Corinthian church, from which Paul was then writing, had objected more strenuously than any other. Money was thus the root of church conflicts, then as now.

The heat of conflict, however, had not induced the apostle to withdraw his request for funds. He had, in fact, made the gathering of this fund one of the tests of the loyalty of the Gentile congregations. He had spent several years at it and had shaped his itinerary to facilitate it. References in five of his letters prove how carefully he planned the solicitation. This was his primary reason for sending his associates back to the communities he had recently established in Macedonia and Achaea. The fund was so large and the

suspicion of dishonesty so great that from the first Paul had
planned to have at least four messengers deliver it. It was at the
moment when these arduous preparations had been completed
that he wrote to the Romans.

But if the gathering of the fund had been hard, its delivery was
even more hazardous. The extent to which Paul was aware of the
risk is clearly proved by this letter. He begs those distant Christians to pray 'that I may be delivered from the unbelievers in
Judea, and that my service for Jerusalem may be acceptable to the
saints' (15.31). Nothing more fully proves the significance of the
fund in Paul's eyes than the fact that he judged its safe delivery to
be worth the risk of his life. The result, in fact, proved how well
his fears were grounded: riot, imprisonment, the journey to
Rome as a prisoner, death in Rome. His life was the price he finally
paid for fulfilling his promise to Peter and James. 'When he
arrived in the city, so full for him of poignant memories, it was to
find the leaders of the church friendly but embarrassed, and a
powerful section prejudiced and embittered' (G. O. Griffith).[1] It
is in fact doubtful if the leaders of the church were so friendly as
Griffith, basing his conclusions on Luke's account in Acts, has
contended. Few ancient letters are so clearly dated: Paul wrote
Romans as he was departing for Jerusalem with money, the collection of which had estranged Gentile Christians and the delivery
of which would antagonize Jewish Christians in Jerusalem (15.25).

These were the circumstances. But why was Paul prompted to
write to Rome? He appealed with great urgency for supporting
prayers from the Roman brothers. To those who discount the
significance of intercessory prayers this may seem a negligible
motive; but not to the apostle. He believed that such prayers could
be of great effect. He also believed that prayers and deeds are
interwoven. He may therefore have expected from them some
action to support their prayers. If so, he left it to them to decide
what should be the form of action, that is, unless Phoebe carried
more exact requests (16.2). Did he want the Romans to exert their
influence over the 'unbelievers in Judea'? This is doubtful,
although by no means impossible. Did he want them to urge 'the
saints' (15.31) to accept Paul's 'service'? This is probable, although
not certain. As we shall see, at least one faction among the Roman
Christians was as hostile to Paul's work as were the Jerusalem
saints. If this faction had kept in close touch with the church in the

Holy City, which is altogether possible, then it would be a strategic gain if Paul could win their support by means of this letter. At any rate, the thesis of the pages which follow is that some Roman congregations represented the kind of Gentile constituency which Paul had alienated in collecting the fund and that other congregations represented the kind of Jewish constituency which would be angered by Paul's delivery of the fund. If that is true, Paul's wishes in collecting and delivering the fund would be directly linked to his desires to reconcile the enemy camps in Rome. Since the problem was the same, the objective would be the same. If the objective could be attained in Rome, it could be attained in Jerusalem. Thus, Paul may have had in mind the same objectives in writing the letter as in delivering the fund.

We should not overlook the important connections between the fund and the early struggle between the Jewish and Gentile wings of the church. It had been at the Jerusalem Council that the apostles had sought to resolve the issues, and one of the items in the resolution had been Paul's pledge to collect this fund. This struggle had begun at least as early as the stoning of Stephen; it would continue at least until the destruction of Jerusalem more than three decades later. In some way the preservation of unity between Jewish and Gentile churches depended upon the delivery of the promised aid (Gal. 2.1–10). Only from this angle does it become clear why Paul was willing to jeopardize the loyalty of his Gentile churches and to risk his own life in carrying through on his earlier commitment to James, Cephas and John. It is not strange that he urged believers in Rome to pray for his success in Jerusalem. E. Fuchs even suggests that The Epistle to the Romans was intended secretly for Jerusalem. Marxsen has better ground for insisting that while Romans was indeed intended for Rome, the problems there were the same as those at Jerusalem.[2] For myself, I would stress the similarity of the struggle in the two cities, but I would go further in stressing the fact of frequent and close communication between the factions in the two cities, so that support for Paul's 'ecumenical mission' in one city would enlarge support in the other as well.

One might summarize the purposes growing directly out of Paul's immediate and long-range plans as follows: He wanted to tell why he had not managed to come to Rome sooner. He wanted to solicit united support for his dangerous mission to Jerusalem and for his later mission to Spain. He knew that before such united support would be possible, the separate Christian groups in Rome must rise above their hostility towards one another. A more specific purpose may have been present in the trip (or mission) of Phoebe to Rome (16.1f.). It is likely that she carried the letter with her. It is therefore possible that she also had oral instructions for securing specific help for Paul from the recipients of the letter.

We turn now to consider what may be uncovered by a more detailed picture of the situation in Rome. An important resource is to be found in 14.1–15.16, and a close scrutiny of those chapters should prove rewarding. Just as the data concerning Paul's personal plans are located at the beginning and at the end of the letter, so, too, we may find there the ground for his concern with the Roman brothers. Although his general desire is mentioned in 1.1–17, his much more specific treatment of the situation is withheld until the closing chapters.

In a sense this leads us to study the letter backwards, inasmuch as we want to know as much as possible about its occasion and purpose, and most of this data is located at the end. Although this may seem to be the wrong way to read a letter, certain compensations may be cited. For example, many studies never reach this point, both teacher and students being exhausted much earlier. Most commentaries give a disproportionate attention to the earlier chapters; Nygren, for example, gives $\frac{1}{25}$ of his space to the last sixth of the text (chs. 14–16).[3] And Nygren is by no means the least balanced of commentators. Valid reasons for the disproportion are apparent. For one thing, the earlier sections are more difficult to comprehend. Moreover, they seem to be more significant. They reveal the theological roots of Paul's thought, whereas the later sections give chiefly the ethical fruits. Students like to go to the roots. Furthermore, the earlier sections are more general, the latter more specific. The earlier have therefore proved less susceptible to the erosions of historical weather than the latter.

Yet some of these reasons for concentrating on the earlier chapters may be dubious. The last few chapters are not so easily understood, as is often supposed, nor so independent of the others, nor so relative and expendable, nor so unimportant theologically. It may prove true that a full understanding of the conclusions of Paul's complex argument is essential for understanding each stage in that argument. If the last chapters give the clearest picture of the situation in Rome, and hence the best clues to purposes and objectives, we may not be able to reconstruct the two-sided conversation between Paul and the Romans at any point in the letter unless we first scrutinize those chapters. We know from his earlier letters how practical and pastoral were Paul's concerns; it would be strange indeed if those concerns were not basic to this letter as well.

One early inference from a close study of chs. 14–16 is extremely important. This is the answer one gives to the question: should we visualize only one congregation in Rome, or several? The habit of commentators, encouraged by the study of Paul's other letters, is to assume the existence of only one parish which met as a unit regularly for common worship. If conflicts are reported, they must have taken place within a single congregation. In that case, as was true in Corinth, the apostle would seek to limit the schism by strengthening an earlier sense of identity and interdependence. A single cell that had emerged from one synagogue or one Gentile home through the initiative of a single leader would be subject to possible splintering. In this case we visualize one practice of baptism which was being disrupted. Almost without exception scholars assume this picture of an earlier unity threatened by a later anarchy (Barrett, Barth, Lietzmann, Marxsen, Nygren, Schlatter, Leenhardt). They visualize a single Christian community where Jewish Christians worshipped side by side with Gentile Christians. On the arrival of Phoebe both factions would listen simultaneously to the letter being read at a single assembly.

Virtually no evidence exists in the letter itself, however, to support this picture of a single congregation. We do not find in Romans the use of the singular in the salutation: 'to the church in . . .', which we find in five other letters (I, II Cor.; I, II Thes.; Philemon). On the contrary, ch. 16 distinguishes at least five or six different house-churches, those of Prisca and Aquila, of Aristobulus, of Asyncritus, of Narcissus, of Philologus. (This point, to be sure, depends upon accepting this chapter as part of the Roman letter, a point which will be defended later in this study.) It is probable that these various cells were brought into existence at diverse times, by diverse leaders, with diverse conceptions of the gospel. Some of them probably antedated the effort of Claudius in AD 49 to destroy the movement, for it is unlikely that his expulsion should have caught all possible culprits. In fact, the disputes described in ch. 14 are such as to have made common meetings impossible. There it is clear that the groups could not agree on holy days, nor could they eat food at the same table. Habitual ridicule and condemnation had frustrated efforts to combine the several congregations. Any apostle who wished to gain the vigorous support of all these cells would need first to produce among them a new sense of interdependence. He would need to replace an anarchic past with a common hope and to redirect centrifugal prejudices and habits towards a new centre.

We should remember the great size of the city of Rome and its polyglot population, which included a large Jewish ghetto, a large number of satellite suburbs, and various neighbourhoods which retained their own ethnic and cultural distinctiveness within the metropolitan area. Among the synagogues the variations in origin were often reflected: e.g. there were synagogues of the Asians, the Judeans, the Achaeans. Instead of visualizing a single Christian congregation, therefore, we should constantly reckon with the probability that within the urban area were to be found forms of Christian community which were as diverse, and probably also as alien, as the churches of Galatia and those of Judea. Consequently, the apostle was attempting within the bounds of a single letter to address them all. We must look very closely then at these various groups. I believe that we may distinguish at least five distinct factions, or, if faction be too strong a word, five different positions.

1. The 'weak in faith' who condemned the 'strong in faith'*

First, let us collect the materials relevant to the identification of this group. By their adversaries they are ridiculed and despised as weak and incompetent (οἱ ἀσθενοῦντες 14.1; οἱ ἀδύνατοι 15.1). The word used to describe weakness was elsewhere used to describe illness (Matt. 25.36; Luke 4.40; 9.2; Phil. 2.26f.). The incompetence is that of men for whom certain actions have become impossible (Rom. 8.3; Luke 18.27). This illness or impotence is viewed by their critics as due to a deficiency in their faith. Their faith was not strong enough to permit them to eat all kinds of food (v. 2), but they condemned as a sinner the Christian who had no scruples

---

* Wherever these terms are used hereafter they should be thought of as partisan labels reflecting Roman prejudice and not as objective designations. The reader should therefore assume that they stand in inverted commas.

whatever over food (v. 3). Their weakness in faith did not enable them to view all days of the week as equally sacred, but they required special reverence for one day, presumably the Sabbath and the festivals. They called down God's curses on every Christian who disobeyed this commandment of the Decalogue. Thus they assumed the right, even the duty, of both defining and enforcing the rules of behaviour for all Christian brothers. This entailed the fixed conviction that some foods were by nature defiling and sinful (14.14). Their ban may have included the drinking of wine (14.21), at least in circumstances determined by the strong in faith. Not only did the weak abstain from certain foods as sinful and observe certain days as holy; their condemnation of their fellows proved that, in their judgment, the Lord would be quite unable to save who did not do likewise (14.4). Thus they heaped a pile of reproaches on the heads of those whom they libelled as lawless and libertine (15.3). The demands of both consistency and legality prevented them from table-fellowship and from common worship with the strong. 'What fellowship can light have with darkness?'

This group was composed largely of converted Jews, but it may have included some Gentiles who, in becoming Christian, had accepted the yoke of the Law. Not all Jewish believers were members, nor were all its members of Jewish descent; but they were all inclined to exalt the 'promises given to the patriarchs' and Christ's service 'to the circumcised' (15.8). This is why they avoided the unkoshered meats of the pagan city and observed the calendar of festivals and Sabbaths. Troubled by the synagogue's rejection of the gospel, they attributed this rejection, at least in part, to the lawlessness of Gentile believers rather than to the blindness and sin of Israel. Before they could attract more Jews to the gospel the Christian cells would need to be purged of scorn for God's Law. Uncleanness must be eradicated; the lawless must be brought into line; Jewish converts must be persuaded not to forfeit their kinship to Abraham and Moses. Thus desire for the salvation of all Christians motivated this group to enforce the norms which for centuries had marked the boundaries between Jew and Gentile, between the righteous and the unrighteous.

Such is the portrait to which the evidence appears to point. There are two statements which seem to contradict this portrait of a party made up primarily of Jews. First is the phrase in 14.2: 'The weak man eats only vegetables.' It is doubtful if many Jews in the first century were vegetarians. How, then, can this definition apply to a group largely Jewish, whose scruples were based on Torah? One reply is this: we are dealing here not with a calm, factual statement but with a slur used by the opposing faction to express scorn. Another reply: the behaviour being described is that of scrupulous Torah readers when they were invited to an integrated dinner in a Gentile house-church. In that circumstance, their only course of action would be to avoid all meat, and in the mind of their Gentile host this would be tantamount to vegetarianism.[4]

The other dubious statement is the phrase in 14.21 which implies that the weak in faith refused to drink wine. Not many Jews had such scruples. What is at stake in this verse, however, is the danger of causing a brother to stumble. Wine would seem to provide such an occasion whenever a Gentile house-church allowed its new-found freedom and exuberance to find expression in what, for a pious Jew, would be a drunken orgy (e.g. 13.13, see below, p. 85). The point is not total abstention from all wine on grounds of conscience, but scrupulous fears of lawless inebriation and of guilt by association with drunken Gentile Christians.

2. *The strong in faith who scorned and despised the weak in faith*

In Rome the situation had become polarized. Each group of adversaries was becoming more frozen in its own position, a position which in turn solidified the extremism of its opponents. One can therefore outline the position of this second group simply by underscoring the antipathies of the first. The group called itself the strong, οἱ δυνατοί, in faith. Their faith enabled them to consider all foods acceptable, to eat anything whether or not it had been banned from the diet of the righteous (14.2, 14). Moreover, they enjoyed wrangling with the scrupulous over this matter (14.1). In fact, they scorned and despised those who were inhibited by laws concerning food (14.3, 10). The word translated *despise* (ἐξουθενέω) indicates angry repudiation, since it is the word often used in the New Testament to describe men's rejection of Jesus (Mark 9.12; Luke 23.11; Acts 4.11). It fitted well a situation where one's self-righteousness was hidden by his pious protest against another's sinfulness (Luke 18.9). It indicated treatment of these fellow-believers as if they were non-persons or nobodies (I Cor. 1.28).

The same freedom from religious taboos extended also to the

calendar. All days are the same, none being more or less sacred than another (14.5). To reject the observance of special days was viewed as a form of giving thanks to God and of honouring the Lord. Had not the Messiah liberated men from the imprisoning bond of such regulations? πάντα καθαρά: all things are clean. (Not unlike the stance of modern Christians who claim that Christ is the end of religion; faith places one in a post-religious era; it enables him to live above and beyond religion.) It is altogether likely that these brothers celebrated the dawn of the kingdom of God by demonstrating radical emancipation from all such pious inhibitions (14.17). They were convinced that this same freedom ought to be displayed by every Christian and should be accepted as the norm for all. Those who did not yet share their freedom should not be welcomed until they had been fully converted. They were ill and must be healed. Ridicule and heated debates thus became a necessary form of therapy.

It is probable that most members of this faction were either uncircumcised Gentiles or Jews who had relished this exhilarating 'post-religious' liberty. As an example, Paul himself, although he was a Jew, identified himself with the strong, except for their scorn of the weak (15.1). Many members doubtless used their emancipation as added justification for pandering to the desires of the flesh. They had not refrained from what their Jewish brothers would consider revelling and drunkenness (13.13). More scrupulous brothers would easily charge them with sinning more wildly in order that grace might abound (6.1). They accepted the declaration, 'no condemnation' (8.1), with exhilaration and joy. It brought such exuberant vitality that they became suspicious of Christians who would try to re-establish old restrictions and obligations. Faith was the source of their strength. The stronger the faith, the greater the freedom from regulations. As W. D. Davies has written: 'Among Gentiles, who lacked any deep acquaintance with Judaism, antinomianism was always crouching at the door ready to enter in under the cloak of grace.'[5]

It is easy to understand why they should despise those weaker than themselves, who could not, for conscience sake, join in their exuberant celebrations. These 'weaklings' must have appeared to be pharisaic prudes, capable only of petty complaints and neurotic fears of contamination. The strong delighted in deriding their squeamishness, in needling them into 'disputes over opinions'.

Nor were they averse to shocking the weak intentionally, posing the offence of the gospel by arrogant indifference to moral restraints. Often by invitation or ridicule they tried to cajole or force the weak into stepping over the line into forbidden territory, getting them to do things still considered unclean. Thus freedom-loving saints destroyed any prospect of genuine harmony or mutual understanding except at the price of capitulation by their enemies.[6]

3. *The doubters*

The description in 14.23 is the key to this group:

> He who has doubts is condemned, if he eats,
> because he does not act from faith.

Paul concedes that the weak in faith may act from faith in observing dietary and calendric regulations, and that the strong in faith may act from faith in treating all foods as clean and all days as being alike. But he knew that it is possible to act without reference to one's own faith, without appeal to one's own conscience, and only in response to social pressures exerted by the dogmatists of either polarized extreme. A brother may decide to eat while he is still uncertain of what the gospel commands. He is vulnerable to the 'disputes over opinions' (14.1), susceptible to the arguments of both strong and weak. In his uncertainty he becomes more fearful of their condemnation or ridicule than of Christ's judgment (14.4); this fear makes him unable to thank God and to hope in him (14.6–9). It is he who is in jeopardy of stumbling, for he might give in to the pressure from the libertarians and eat food which he still believed unclean (14.13–16). In other situations and in Paul's other letters, the doubters seem largely to have been Gentiles who were tempted to seek the double safety of legal righteousness in order to diminish their guilt (cf. Gal. 5). But in Rome, as also in the Gentile church at Corinth (I Cor. 8.9–13; 10.14–30), it was Jewish Christians who stood in the greater danger (although of danger from the other side, cf. below, pp. 79f.). Uncertain of how much they should observe the Torah, secretly enamoured of the freedoms enjoyed by the 'strong', fearful of being ostracized by the weak and of being cursed by God, yet responsive to the apostolic announcements of emancipation, they were far from clear in their own mind about what was right for them (14.5).

It was from the ranks of the doubters that both weak and strong sought to enlist recruits. The enlistment of a doubter registered a victory for one side, but this only served to escalate the war. Paul saw both continued wavering and hurried endorsement of the 'strong' as fatal misunderstandings of the gospel. So long as action sprang from something other than faith, it was sinful and it entailed God's condemnation (14.23). Paul appeared to be more concerned with the danger of ruin to these doubters than about all the other parties to the conflict (14.15). This concern focused his attention on those who might cause such ruin, and it is to them that Paul addressed his arguments. What they considered a vindication of the truth of their position, Paul views as a destruction of the work of God (14.20). What to them was a token of the presence of the kingdom of God was to Paul its denial (14.17).

4. *The weak in faith who did not condemn the strong*

The crucial issue which alienated the Roman congregations was not the choice of foods or days, but the attitude towards those who made a contrary choice. The determination of one's own behaviour was one thing; the judgment of those who differed was another. Consider the weak in faith. There were two groups, distinguished by whether or not they condemned 'the servant of another' (14.4). The apostle adopted very different ways of dealing with these two groups. He did not try to persuade the weak to relax their dietary or calendric scruples. He did not attack those scruples as wrong; in fact, he endorsed them. Meat, he wrote, 'is unclean for anyone who thinks it unclean' (14.14). Yet he did repudiate in no uncertain terms the presumption by the weak of their right to dictate the duties of other Christians and to judge their holiness before God. Such dictation and such judgment were direct denials of the property rights of God and of the power of Christ (14.3f., 10–12). And there were some Christians in Rome who agreed with Paul, who themselves observed the Decalogue rule on the Sabbath and the various regulations of diet without condemning the strong in faith or demanding that the strong live as they did. They were content to keep their faith as a matter between themselves and God (14.22). Their energies were directed towards honouring and thanking the Lord, towards rejoicing in the Lord's power (14.6–9), towards celebrating the presence of the kingdom in peace, joy, mutual up-building (14.17–19), towards joining in the fulfilment of the promises to the patriarchs by praising God with the strong in faith (15.7–12). There is ample evidence of the wholesome presence of this group among the Roman congregations. It is clear that Paul welcomed their aid in the fulfilment of his own objectives, although, in the nature of the case, he did not directly address them, except perhaps in ch. 16 (cf. below, pp. 24f.).

5. *The strong in faith who did not despise the weak*

In the tangled Roman situation, Groups One and Two* were bound by their very antagonisms to aggravate the cleavage, making each other more intransigent and steadily increasing the pressures on the doubters. Groups Four and Five, by contrast, were bound to move towards each other, to accentuate mutual bonds and to reduce the danger of ruin to the doubters. Paul was hoping to find stauch reinforcement in both these groups. The chief threat to all of his objectives was located in Groups One and Two. The success of his letter, as well as of his projected visit and mission to Spain, depended upon persuading members of those groups to shift to Groups Four or Five. It is almost certain that Gentile Christians were in the majority among the churches of Rome and that this letter is more strongly slanted towards them. It is certain that it was their negative attitudes towards the Torah which had sparked the fires of conflict among the scattered congregations, and that those attitudes exerted strong pressures on the doubters (Group Three). Paul was especially desirous, therefore, of changing their entrenched attitudes and actions.

It is essential to note, however, how fully the apostle agreed with their programmatic declarations. 'Nothing is unclean in itself' (14.14); 'Everything is clean' (14.20). 'He who eats, eats in honour of the Lord' (14.6). It was their condescension towards the weak, together with the influence of their examples and their debates on the doubters, which Paul attacks. As Paul saw the problem, it was not only possible but essential for the strong in faith, without compromising the truth of their convictions, to extend perfect hospitality to the weak (14.1), to forego endless

* Later in this study, in the interest of saving space and avoiding repetition, I will refer to these five groups by number. As each reference appears the reader is urged to recall the whole definition as given in these pages. Such a reminder will prevent him from visualizing these partisan groups as if they were highly organized and cohesive entities.

quarrels over food and holy days, to avoid supercilious scorn (14.3), to acknowledge God's acceptance of the weak, to bear their failings, if need be, to accept their reproaches (15.1–3), and to join gratefully in perfect harmony within the new regime in which Jews and Gentiles are ruled by the same Lord (15.12). Already when Paul wrote, there were among Roman Christians such representatives of the strong in faith. By writing, Paul hoped to increase the number of the strong who insisted that the strong had no right to require that the weak live like them.[7]

It is in ch. 15 that we see most clearly the extent to which Paul hoped to increase the numbers of Roman Christians who would come to belong to Group Four or Five. He did not expect to combine these two groups into one by persuading all to have the same conscience vis-à-vis foods and days. To have attempted that goal would have been futile. Or, what was more decisive to Paul, such an attempt would have been sinful. The genuine and necessary goal of faith required that these groups should welcome one another even while they held opposing views on foods and days (15.7). The measure of this welcome had already been established: 'As Christ has welcomed you.' Clear also was the motivation of this welcome: 'For the glory of God.'

How had Christ welcomed them? The answer is quite clear and entirely cogent. 'The reproaches of those who reproached thee fell on me' (15.3, a quotation of Ps. 69.19). The reproaches and the condemnations which righteous Jews, obedient to the Law, had heaped upon the unrighteous (publicans, harlots, demon-possessed, Gentiles) had fallen on Jesus. In being condemned by the weak in faith, the strong in faith had been sharing in the fate of Jesus. They had been put in the position where they could fully understand the saving work of Jesus. Jesus had accepted the burden of all these reproaches as the means by which he could deliver men from condemnation. Jesus had done this not to please himself, but to save both those who reproached and those who were reproached. Thus his action had become the standard which should be adopted by the strong in faith. 'Christ did not please himself' (15.1). All actions towards the weak in faith and towards the doubters must be controlled by the same motives: 'not to please ourselves'. Did the weak reproach the strong? Christ had accepted such reproaches for the sake of the weak. Did the strong reproach the weak? Christ had borne those failings as well.

Wherever Christians treated other Christians with condemnation or ridicule, the recipient of their reproaches was the Lord to whom the others belonged. Each Christian, then, was a person whose reproach Christ had borne. Now, in his attitude towards other believers, he either added to the reproaches of Christ or he joined Christ in bearing reproaches. That appears to be the logic of the situation.

Two important paragraphs in the first half of ch. 15 serve as the climax of Paul's appeal. Verses 1–6 are directed mainly at Group Two, with which Paul establishes a limited identity for the purpose of winning members over into Group Five. The benediction of vv. 5f. provides an apt summary of that appeal. Verses 7–13 are addressed to Groups One and Two together; this address also concludes with an appropriate benediction. In this section Paul also reminds his readers of the character of Christ's work. In the wisdom of God, he insists, Christ made the salvation promised to the Jews (the weak in faith) absolutely contingent upon the inclusion of the Gentiles. For this reason the weak in faith must praise God for *and with* the strong. Notice the logical sequence:

(*a*) 'Christ became a servant to the circumcised . . .
(*b*) in order that Gentiles might glorify God for his mercy. . . .
(*c*) Therefore, I [a Jew] will praise thee *among the Gentiles*. . . .'

The same logic also locks the Gentile Christians (the strong in faith) into the same redemptive triangle:

(*a*) 'In order that Gentiles might glorify God for his mercy . . .
(*b*) Christ became a servant to the circumcised. . . .
(*c*) [Therefore] rejoice, O Gentiles *with his people*.'

Because of the work of Christ, 'the root of Jesse' (in confirmation of God's promises to the patriarchs) has come as a ruler of both Jews and Gentiles. Therefore, faith that is genuine is marked by joy and peace, not by mutual recrimination. The strength of faith is to be measured not by a man's ability to eat all foods but by the power of the Holy Spirit, a power which conveys an abundant share in God's hope. It was this strength which Paul wanted to convey to both strong and weak in Rome. If he were successful in that effort, Group Four would win recruits from Group One, Group Five from Group Two, the danger to Group Three would be reduced, and a larger number of segregated house-churches would at last be able to worship together – Jews praising God among the Gentiles and Gentiles praising God with his people (15.9f.). When that goal was accomplished in Rome, Paul believed that the 'offering of the Gentiles' would be acceptable and his assignment in 'the priestly service of the gospel of God' would be accomplished (15.16).

There is another way to summarize Paul's objectives in his confrontation with Groups One and Two. One can collect those axioms which are sprinkled through chs. 14 and 15, which Paul saw as belonging to the essentials of the gospel, which had, at least, in part, been accepted by the last two groups and which Paul wanted to use as the basis for reconciliation of the first two groups. These axioms formed the pivots of his appeals to the Romans. If these were seen as valid, his appeals would stand; if invalid, they would fall. If he could convince his readers of their truth, this accomplishment should in itself overcome their hostilities; if not, the conflicts would continue unmitigated. Having distinguished the five positions, let us concentrate on these fundamental convictions of Christian faith which Paul saw as being jeopardized by the bickering in Rome.

In the first paragraph of ch. 14 (vv. 1–4) there are several *descriptive* statements, which we may assume to be based on reports from Rome, e.g. 'One believes he may eat anything.' There follow *hortatory* appeals by which the apostle urged a change in behaviour, e.g. 'As for the man who is weak in faith, welcome him.' Finally, there are *assertions* on which those appeals are grounded. Let us notice those assertions.

Axiom 1: 'God has welcomed him' (the man who eats).
Axiom 2: Only the Master can judge his servant (paraphrase of v. 4b).
Axiom 3: That servant will be upheld, for the Master has power to uphold him.

By condemning the strong, the weak in faith denied each of these assertions. So, too, did the strong in faith, when they despised the weak. Although these denials may have been unconscious and implicit, they were none the less real. Paul's case, therefore, depended upon clinching the truth of these contentions, a truth by no means self-evident, then or now. Yet the apostle did not attempt here to accomplish that clinching. In subsequent chapters we shall try to show how that had already been accomplished earlier in chs. 1–11.

In the second paragraph (14.5–9), we notice again two types of statement: exhortations ('Let every one be fully convinced') and descriptions ('He who observes the day observes it in honour of the Lord'). We notice also that these descriptions now focus upon the intention which characterizes the mind of both strong and weak. Paul sees that both of their diverse types of behaviour seek to give thanks to God and to honour the Lord. Both have entered into covenant with God by making the simplest and most basic of all confessions: Jesus is Lord. So Paul set forth the axiomatic truth concerning their common relationship to Christ:

Axiom 4: He is 'Lord both of the dead and the living' (v. 9).

Again we note that this assertion is not self-evident and that in this context Paul did not attempt to defend it.

In the third paragraph (14.10–12) Paul allowed two rhetorical questions to serve both a descriptive and hortatory function. The accompanying axiom appears twice (vv. 10c, 12):

Axiom 5: 'Each of us shall give account of himself to God',

the two instances being separated by a citation of scripture to support the axiom.

In the next paragraph (14.13–23) there is more frequent and confusing alternation between exhortation, description and assertion. Even so, the assertions remain pivotal to the argument. Thus the command of v. 13 is based upon the compound assertion in v. 14.

Axiom 6a: 'Nothing is unclean in itself,
    6b: but it is unclean for any one who thinks it unclean.'

In this couplet the apostle adeptly combined the convictions of opposing factions. The first line was the catchword of Group One, the second took account of the cry of Group Two. By combining the two axioms into one, the apostle risked alienating both in his effort to agree with both. Neither would accept without further argument Paul's linking of the objective truth with the subjective. The same basic command is supported by the same basic axiom in v. 20, except for the second line of the couplet:

Axiom 7a: 'Everything is indeed clean,
      7b: but it is wrong for anyone to make others fall by what he eats.'

I have called this a separate axiom because of its second line. When this second line is linked to the second line of Axiom 6, we locate an implicit presupposition of Paul's thought, which not only was ignored by the strong in faith but also is rejected by most modern readers:

Axiom 8: 'When one is persuaded to eat food which he believes to be unclean, he is caused to fall.'

Interspersed in the text are several alternate ways of evaluating this fall: it is a matter of stumbling (v. 13), injury (v. 15), ruin (v. 15), destroying the work of God (v. 20), condemnation (v. 23). At this point, at least, Paul agreed with the weak in faith; he recognized the dangers of total loss which were involved in the quarrels in Rome. Thinking of this loss as occasioned by the pressures exerted on the doubters by the strong in faith, he made two assertions which were axiomatic with him, though not with them.

Axiom 9: 'If your brother is being injured by what you eat, you are no longer walking in love' (v. 15).
Axiom 10: 'Happy is the man who does not bring God's condemnation on himself by doing what he considers right' (my translation).

Both groups had allowed themselves to become obsessed with such matters as dietary regulations and with mutual recriminations. Both had allowed their obsessions to distort their understandings of the power and the nature of God's kingdom. Paul's thought rotated around a quite different conception:

Axiom 11: 'The kingdom of God is not eating and drinking but righteousness, peace and joy in the Holy Spirit' (v. 17, my translation).

Perhaps the most abrasive element of all conflicts in Rome was the idea of sin implicit in the interpersonal judging process. To the weak, the strong were sinners who falsely claimed the justification of Christ's freedom. To the strong, the weak were made sinners by their refusal to allow Christ to free them from their tight legalisms.

To Paul, both were assuming a pre-conversion idea of sin, an idea which should have been basically corrected by the gospel. Against both groups, he set his own conviction concerning the detection and cure of sin:

> *Axiom 12*: 'Sin is whatever does not proceed from faith' (v. 23, my translation).

Here we touch upon a conviction which requires the whole epistle to articulate and to sustain it. What is it which proceeds from faith? What does not so proceed? All the readers had faith (1.8); all gave thanks to God and honoured the Lord (14.6). Yet not all kept this faith between themselves and God (14.22); not all measured sin by this faith. Each was more eager to detect his brother's sin than his own, establishing his own behaviour as norm and then trying to enforce that norm on the others. Each assumed that such dictatorial enforcement of 'righteousness' proceeded from faith and was required by it. Each assumed that the strength of his faith was to be measured by the success of such a procedure. Axiom 12 serves to locate this issue but not to establish the answer. How may we surely determine what does or does not proceed from faith? How may we correctly measure the strength of our own faith? How is faith itself to be strengthened? In the following chapters we shall survey some of the ways in which the apostle sought to convince the Roman congregations of the validity of these twelve axioms and we shall undertake to answer the questions noted above.

Before we proceed to the study of the epistle from this point of view, we should stop to consider three possible objections to this approach. The first has to do with doubts as to whether chs. 14 and 15 were actually based on information from Rome. Did Paul, in Corinth, have accessible so detailed a knowledge of the situation in Rome? Should we not rather treat these chapters as presenting stock answers to typical problems which arose in all Gentile congregations? May they not reflect the quarrels in Corinth where Paul knew the situation, rather than in Rome, where he did not?

In the nature of the case there can be no certain removal of these doubts; scholars' own predispositions will lead them to opposite conclusions. Two judgments are typical of what appears in many commentaries:

Professor Dodd writes:

From the epistle itself we can learn little about the Roman church. Unlike other epistles, it has no particular reference to the internal conditions of the church to which it is addressed, and Paul has no direct acquaintance with them.[8]

Professor Leenhardt makes much the same point:

Paul is not really addressing a particular group of people, whose concrete circumstances he is considering while pointing out their errors. . . . In spite of certain appearances Paul is not here concerned to remonstrate with Christians at Rome, whom he does not know any more than he knows their special problems. . . . The problem which the apostle is treating . . . is a practical problem which he is treating theoretically and abstractly.[9]

We can be absolutely sure of one thing only: Paul had never been at Rome and whatever information he had must have reached him through other Christians. But there are considerations which persuade me that Dodd and Leenhardt are wrong. We know that Prisca and Aquila had come from Rome, after being expelled under Claudius, probably because they had been among the Christians causing controversy among the synagogues. Paul had worked many years with them. They would surely have briefed him about conditions and persons in Rome up until the time of their eviction. Moreover, if we can treat ch. 16 as part of the original letter, we can conclude that this brave couple had returned to Rome. If so, they would almost certainly have kept in touch by letter or messenger with the apostle and with the churches in Corinth and Ephesus. We shall soon return to the problem of ch. 16. If it is part of the original letter, then it is evident that Paul knew many others also who had gone to Rome, with whom he had probably kept in touch.

Consider, too, some of the inferences to be drawn from 15.14–33. For a long while the apostle had been planning a trip to Rome and Spain. Such a trip required preparation well in advance. It is altogether likely, therefore, that he would have solicited every bit of information he could secure about conditions in Rome. We know that communication was very frequent between Paul and many other cities – in Galatia, Macedonia, Achaea, and Judea – communication both by person and letter. Why should Rome be excluded from that list? There is no good reason. The probability of acquaintance with the situation is strengthened when one observes certain literary factors. The section, 15.14–33, certainly assumes both a concern for the situation in Rome and some knowledge of it. While in some ways distinct, it is a direct sequel to the thought of 15.1–13 (e.g. the relation between Gentiles and Jews in the providence of God and in Paul's vocational strategy, the mutual indebtedness of Jews and Gentiles, the weak and strong in faith). This earlier section, in turn, is inseparable in its address and argumentation from ch. 14. Paul's knowledge of the Roman situation, as exemplified at the end of ch. 15, is therefore continuous with the knowledge at the beginning of ch. 14.

It is true that Paul often incorporated into his letters didactic material which was typical of what he taught in all the churches. This catechetical material was often shaped by general practice rather than by particular situations. Chapters 12 and 13 contain material which is probably of this sort (see below, however, for important qualifications, pp. 82–90.) There is, however, a change in literary style between ch. 13 and 14.[10] The apostle moves from general injunctions, embodied in traditional oral forms of parenesis, to the consideration of a specific set of problems. The nearest analogy is I Corinthians (8.1–13; 9.19–23; 10.23–11.1). No one doubts that in Corinth he was wrestling directly with a specific situation. Why then should we doubt that this was also true in Rome?

The justification of our approach depends finally upon our treatment of the whole letter. If one is convinced that the entire argument is aimed at this situation, he will surely agree that the problems broached in chs. 14 and 15 were more than theoretical.

The second question deals with whether ch. 16 can be used for data on the situation in Rome. Although it is generally accepted that Paul wrote the chapter (apart from the much contested doxology, vv. 25–27), there are many prominent scholars who believe it was written to the church at Ephesus and only later was it appended to the Epistle to the Romans. They have textual evidence to support the existence of Romans without this chapter, although it is primarily their inferences from internal evidence that lead them to deny that this chapter belonged originally to Romans. In any case, the arguments *pro* and *con* are very evenly balanced. I have no wish to review the whole debate or to repeat the argument on both sides. I am concerned with only one area – the issue of possible continuity between the debate of chs. 14, 15 and the data of ch. 16. This is vital to the question of literary integrity, since those who disjoin ch. 16 do so because in that chapter Paul presupposes an intimate, detailed knowledge of members of the community which is not, they believe, presupposed in chs. 1–15. I am convinced that this inference is wrong and that there are very important links to be discerned. I would grant, however, that these links are anything but obvious.

Let us divide the contested chapter into five distinct sections.

1. *A recommendation for Phoebe*

I commend to you our sister Phoebe, a deaconess of the church at Cenchreae, that you may receive her in the Lord as befits the saints, and help her in whatever she may require from you for she has been a helper of many and of myself as well (16.1–2).

Did this double request have any connection with the controversies of chs. 14 and 15 ? It may have; but if so, neither Phoebe nor the Romans would need to have that connection described. We are left, then, with conjecture. What picture emerges from conjecture?

Phoebe carried the letter with her to Rome, where she would take it from one house-church to another, to congregations where the weak in faith were dominant, as well as to others whose members were the strong in faith. The reception which these churches gave to Phoebe would be a test of their reception of the letter. Especially was this true for members of Group One, for Phoebe was a Gentile, whom, nevertheless, Paul called a sister. As an officer in the Gentile church at Cenchreae, she might not be welcomed by Jewish Christians in Rome, if, as is probable, a welcome (v. 2) entailed inclusion at the eucharistic table. Their welcome to Phoebe may be as problematic as the welcome commanded in 14.1; 15.7. If so, this mention of Phoebe was much more than an incidental matter, since the full acceptance of Phoebe would signal their later attitude towards Paul (15.24). Such acceptance would be a measure of their understanding of the letter and their obedience to it, a measure of the extent to which harmony and peace could be made to prevail over divisions.

Paul commanded the readers not only to welcome her but also to help her. In the past Phoebe had helped many, both Gentiles and such Jews as Paul. She would presumably continue doing so in Rome as a deaconess. But now she was coming to the scattered and hostile congregations in Rome and was asking specific help in a very specific business. What was this business? Would it have been her own private occupation? It was more probably to be Christian business. Did it include preparations for Paul's work in Spain? Paul made it a habit to co-opt many helpers on his staff. At the moment a rather large delegation was going to Jerusalem with him. Did Phoebe's role include asking the Romans to join in the contributions to Jerusalem? As Gentile Christians were they included in the pact which he had made with the other apostles (12.13)? Did Phoebe have a special assignment in trying to bring the scattered Roman cells into closer contact with each other? Would she be able to present more fully and directly the reasons for mutual acceptance which Paul had set forth in earlier sections of the letter? This is only conjecture, but it is by no means an implausible deduction. Paul may well have sent Phoebe on this trip hoping that she could implement some of his own purposes. After all, most of the available men seem to have been assigned to the excursion to Judea.

2. *Greetings to individuals in the Roman congregations (16.3–16)*

Greet Prisca and Aquila, my fellow-workers in Christ Jesus, who risked their necks for my life, to whom not only I but also all the churches of the Gentiles give thanks; greet also the church in their house (16.3–5a).

We have already noted that the mention of this one church implies that there were other churches in Rome. We may also infer that these other churches may have been either ignorant of or hostile towards these veteran Christian leaders. Phoebe was a Gentile to whom Jewish Christians were indebted; Aquila was a Jew (Acts 18.2) to whom 'all the churches of the Gentiles give thanks'. Paul makes this very clear. In fact, we need to inquire why Paul should say exactly what he says about this couple when there were so many other things that might have been said on the basis of several years of close co-operation.

We can at least surmise that this man and his wife were well fitted to represent Group Four because of their years of congenial work with Paul. Should it be true that Prisca (Priscilla in Acts) was a wealthy *Gentile* lady from a prominent Roman family, then they would also have been fitted to represent Group Five. They would also be able to support Paul's appeal to Groups One and Two because of their contacts with both the synagogues and the Gentile churches. More than this, they had proved their mettle in danger-ous efforts to save Paul's life. Were there some congregations in Rome which would have scruples against welcoming Prisca and Aquila? It is altogether likely. If so, Paul appeals to them to change their policy. Both by their work in Corinth and Ephesus and by their co-operation with Paul, they had demonstrated how crucial was the interdependence of Jews and Gentiles. We sug-gested earlier that Paul may have received from Prisca and Aquila reports about the situation in Rome. We now suggest that Paul named them first because he was counting heavily on them to deal with the turbulent situation in Rome. After they had returned to Rome, there would be no others in Rome so well acquainted with Paul's policy and so highly trusted by him. Paul would indeed be happy if the other house-churches in Rome should decide on the basis of his letter to accord greater status to this particular congre-gation. This comment supports and extends the suggestion of O. Michel that the return of Prisca and Aquila to Rome had been decided upon in connection with Paul's own plans.[11] The com-mand to salute or to greet them may therefore have been tanta-mount to a number of urgent requests: 'Treat them as you would treat me.' 'Thank them for their service to Gentile churches.' 'Welcome them into your eucharistic fellowship.' 'Respect their judgment and accede to their authority.' 'Support them as they gather resources for my trip to Spain.'

Greet my beloved Epaenetus, who was the first convert of Asia for Christ. Greet Mary who has worked hard among you (16.5b, 6).

Paul continues to alternate between Gentiles and Jews, between men and women, between workers who had begun their disciple-ship abroad and those who had established their merit in Rome. He also probably alternated between those whom he had met (I agree with W. G. Kümmel in listing nine whom Paul must have met in the East: Prisca, Aquila, Epaenetus, Andronicus, Junias, Ampliatus, Stachys, Rufus and his mother)[12] and those in Rome of whom he had only heard, but on whom he could count to help reduce the tension and prepare for the Spanish mission. This alternation bespeaks Paul's care in writing this chapter, care to present those persons and those facts which would contribute to the elimination of ridicule of the weak by the strong and of the condemnation of the strong by the weak.

Epaenetus is recommended as the 'first convert in Asia', much loved by Paul. As such he could represent the Asian churches as well as their founder. He, as well as others mentioned in the chapter, may have been sent from Ephesus in connection with Paul's projected trip. We should not forget that before Paul left Ephesus for Achaea (where he wrote Romans) he was actively contemplating the opening of a mission in new areas (I Cor. 16.4, 6). For the Roman congregations to welcome this Gentile would indicate their later support for the campaign in Spain.

> Greet Andronicus and Junias, my kinsmen and my fellow-prisoners; they are men of note among the apostles, and they were in Christ before me (16.7).

Granted a situation in Rome such as we have pictured, one may imagine various reasons which may have led Paul to stress these facts about these two Jews. To the weak in faith they would carry apostolic authority; moreover, as senior apostles to Paul, they could correct any notion that Paul alone was responsible for his policy of approving full liberty for Gentile believers. To the strong in faith these Jews had proved their courage under fire. It would have been quite wrong to dub them as weaklings. To allow matters of dietary scruples to become more important than apostolic accreditation and bravery under fire would have been ridiculous. Such men as these were qualified to be especially effective in reconciling the alien groups in Rome, and in preparing the churches for Paul's push westward.

> Greet Ampliatus, my beloved in the Lord. Greet Urbanus, our fellow-worker in Christ, and my beloved Stachys.
> Greet Appelles, who is approved in Christ.
> Greet those who belong to the family of Aristobulus.
> Greet my kinsman Herodion.
> Greet those in the Lord who belong to the family of Narcissus.
> Greet those workers in the Lord, Tryphaena and Tryphosa.
> Greet the beloved Persis, who has worked hard in the Lord.
> Greet Rufus, eminent in the Lord, also his mother and mine.
> Greet Asyncritus, Phlegon, Hermes, Patrobas, Hermas and the brethren who are with them.
> Greet Philologus, Julia, Nereus and his sister, and Olympas and all the saints who are with them.
> Greet one another with a holy kiss.
> All the churches of Christ greet you (16.8–16).

This long list, unparalleled in the other letters, calls for some explanation. Why so many names?[13] For one thing, they may have been needed because there were so many scattered house-churches in greater Rome, many of which were isolated either by distance, by ethnic background or by hostility. For another, they may have represented the list of leaders on whom Paul could call for assistance in allaying hostilities. They may have constituted the known members of Groups Four and Five. If the conflicting factions could be persuaded to trust these men and women, they would be well along the road towards mutual respect and co-operation. 'Greet one another with a holy kiss' may have been a very germane command, since, as in I Peter 5.14, we are dealing with scattered congregations, ill-acquainted and given to mutual suspicion. '*All* the churches greet you' may have been an appeal for the recipients to broaden their welcome to include all the churches.

When we ask what accent recurs most frequently in this list, the answer is clear: 'for Christ', 'in Christ', 'in the Lord', 'of Christ'. This is a typically Pauline accent, so much a cliché that we all too easily discount its force. In this context, however, these phrases embody the same logic as the similar phrases which recur so frequently in chs. 14 and 15. Groups One to Three were all characterized by their limitation of the phrase 'in Christ' to friends who agreed with them on holy days and foods. In short, the long list of salutations may well have been a continuation of Paul's appeal for support (in 15.14–33), and a buttress of his arguments with the strong and weak (in 14.1–15.13). This is conjecture, to be sure, but such a conjecture is inherently reasonable.

3. *The harsh warning against divisive leaders*

I appeal to you, brethren, to take note of those who create dissensions and difficulties, in opposition to the doctrine which you have been taught; avoid them. For such persons do not serve our Lord Christ, but their own appetites, and by fair and flattering words they deceive the hearts of the simple-minded. For while your obedience is known to all, so that I rejoice over you, I would have you wise as to what is good and guileless as to what is evil; then the God of peace will soon crush Satan under your feet (16.17–20a).

These verses seem to strike a note in sharpest contrast to the irenic tone of the previous salutations. So sharp is the shift in

mood that many commentators have doubted whether this paragraph could have been addressed to Roman Christians over whom
Paul asserted no authority. This attack on schismatics 'is not in
harmony with the calm and carefully restrained tone of the
epistle'.[14] Many scholars doubt whether Barth was right when he
found in this scathing warning 'the whole polemic of the epistle
. . . concentrated in one blow'.[15]

One can only speculate about the reasons for the apparent shift
in mood. If, however, we have made a good guess as to the reasons
for the long list of salutations, that guess should carry implications
for this immediate sequel. In the salutations Paul was primarily
concerned with the quarrels which had alienated the Roman congregations and with commending those leaders whose teaching
and example would lead to greater harmony. His mind may have
moved directly from this group of trusted leaders to those leaders
whose teaching and example must be shunned. It may have been
the same issue which required him to deal first with those whom
he trusted and then with those whom he feared. His attention
remained fixed on his major objective – the securing of peace
(14.19; 15.5). Given this interpretation, we find no sudden shift
at all.

The description of the false leaders in vv. 17f. fits precisely
Groups One and Two: 'dissensions and difficulties'. The first of
these terms, dissensions, covers the 'disputes over opinions'
(14.1), the ridicule and scorn towards the weak, the condemnation
of the strong, the resulting inability of Christians to eat and to
worship together. These attitudes were certainly in contradiction
(in Paul's mind, at least) to the 'doctrine' which they had learned.
The second of these terms, difficulties, is too mild an English
word to match the force of the Greek word σκάνδαλα. These
stumblings were a result of the bickering, the nasty recriminations,
the endless debating – a result that took the form of the ruin of the
doubters (14.13). Those who were convinced in their own minds
had succeeded in persuading a number of doubters to act in a
manner contrary to their own conscience. The sharp language
merely reflects Paul's high estimate of the terrible cost of this
injury: the destruction of the work of God, the ruin of one for
whom Christ died (14.15, 20). When one takes seriously the blunt
language Paul used in ch.14, it is wrong to say that 16.17–20
replaces an irenic tone by a harsh polemicism. The explicit con-

demnation in 16.17–20 is no stronger than the implicit condemnation in 14.13–23 (or in 2.1–24, below, pp. 49f.).

'Such persons serve their own *appetites*'. . . . This clearly recalls the bitter debates over foods and the assumption that the presence of God's kingdom should be measured by the degree of freedom to eat anything, or contrariwise, by care to obey the scriptural regulations (14.17). 'By fair and flattering words they deceive the hearts of the *simple-minded*.' I believe that these 'simple-minded' represent the doubters and waverers of ch. 14, those who were not clear in their own minds on the issues at stake and who therefore did not act from faith (14.23). In Paul's judgment, Satan was particularly adept in luring the strong in faith into a false sophistication concerning good and evil. For example, rightly persuaded that all foods were clean ('wise as to what is good') they wrongly justified their superiority and scorn of those who were not so wise; they were thus trapped by the good into doing evil. To become aware of such self-deception would be to 'crush Satan under your feet'. It would be foolish to insist that this is the only way to interpret this harsh warning in vv. 17–20, but it would be even more foolish not to reckon with the possibility that the apostle here condensed the pastoral polemic, which had absorbed his thought at least since 14.1, into a last warning, perhaps in his own hand rather than Tertius'. Since Paul was concerned above all with the divisions among Roman brothers, it is natural that he should confront them with the choice between the God of peace (16.20, cf. 15.5, 13, 33) and God's enemy, Satan, the father of divisions. An 'obedience to the faith' which took the form of living 'in harmony with one another, in accord with Christ Jesus' (15.5), would serve to crush Satan 'under your feet' and thus would become an enactment of the redemption promised in Gen. 3.15.[16]

4. *Greetings from Corinth* (16.21–23)

This material is so brief and so conventional that it offers no additional light on the purposes of Paul. It makes clear, however, that Jews (Lucius, Jason, Sosipater) and Gentiles (Gaius, Erastus, Quartus) were co-operating in the conversation and were members of a single congregation. They added their support, tacitly at least, to the position paper which Paul was sending to Rome. Moreover, in sharp contrast to the Roman situation, there was a single church in Corinth which could meet in the house of a single host. In spite of its possession of many explosive gifts, this church had achieved a unity which was yet to be attained in Rome. To be sure, the eucharistic table and the day of worship in Corinth had been scenes of great turbulence, but even that was preferable to the more anarchic situation in Rome.

5. *The doxology* (16.25–27)

Textual problems, along with stylistic and theological features, have led most scholars to doubt that this doxology was Pauline in origin and/or that it was a part of the original copy of Romans. This doubt may be fully justified. It is so well-grounded that I do not wish to base any conclusions about the purposes of Romans on the thesis of its belonging to the epistle. Should the doxology be accepted on other grounds, however, the following observations would become relevant.

Now to him who has the power to strengthen you (in faith) according to my gospel and the preaching of Jesus Christ. . . . (My translation.)

The whole issue in the Roman congregations was the question of how strength of faith was to be measured and secured. The words: faith, strengthen, power, constituted bones of contention. Moreover, to Paul, faith and its strengthening have a single ultimate source: God.

according to the revelation of the mystery which was kept secret for long ages but is now disclosed and through the prophetic writings is made known . . .

In 15.1–13, the apostle had grounded his argument ultimately in the promises to the patriarchs and the scriptures, but he also had given full weight to the new situation in which those promises had been fulfilled by the inclusion of the Gentiles. The secret had, in fact, been well kept for long ages. The union of Jews and Gentiles had long been a genuine mystery (11.25), but it had now been revealed and disclosed through the prophetic writings (including those cited in 15.3–12).

to all Gentiles, according to the command of the eternal God, to bring about the obedience of faith[17] (my translation).

We have elsewhere suggested that Paul's central goal in the epistle was expressed as that of bringing about the obedience of faith, that he accepted this responsibility primarily for the Gentiles (15.16), and that he interpreted this mission as one directly commanded by God.

to the only wise God be glory for evermore through Jesus Christ. Amen.

I believe that this doxology to the wisdom of God may fulfil the same function in chs. 14–16 that the paean of praise in 11.33–36 fulfils in chs. 9–11. The salvation of Jews and Gentiles, the realization of peace among them within one kingdom, was proof for Paul that God alone is wise. Men could not have produced such wisdom. The goal of this harmony between Jew and Gentile, weak and strong, was 'that together you may with one voice glorify the God . . .' (15.6). This closing doxology is thus a virtual repetition of the poetic stanza in 14.7–9, which was itself a summary of the axioms so central to the whole argument. Should the inclusion of this doxology be determined solely by its internal consistency with the rest of the epistle, I would defend the proposition that it formed the original conclusion to the original document.[18]

There is now a third objection to our basic interpretation of chs. 14 and 15, which should be mentioned. Many readers of the epistle are convinced that the problems which Paul discussed there are unimportant, so marginal indeed as to be trivial in comparison to the major themes of the epistle. Many scholars express this judgment silently simply by ignoring these chapters. Others are much more explicit. C. H. Dodd is typical of many Protestant commentators in reducing the issues to 'sabbatarianism' and 'vegetarianism' and by dubbing these matters 'fads'. As fads, their only basis is 'opinions and prejudices which, though sincerely held, have no rational ground, but are of the nature of taboo'. In the modern situation only a few disputes may be considered comparable, such as the Puritan Sunday and fish during Lent. Although temporarily the liberated must respect the prudish, the ultimate solution is for the prudes to surrender their irrational taboos. In the interim, such things are 'tiresome questions . . . which may easily split a church' but they can be readily solved by rational appeals to the example of Christ. Thus far Professor Dodd.[19] Typical of many Catholic commentators is A. Wikenhauser's brief dismissal of the problems discussed in 14.1–15.13: 'The point at issue there is not fundamental.' I believe that there is a double thrust in Wikenhauser's judgments: he means that neither was the point at issue fundamental in the ancient situation, whether for Paul or for the Roman brothers, nor is it fundamental today. What was and is fundamental in the Epistle to the Romans are such things as the relation between faith and works, between justification and the Law, and 'the destiny of the Jewish people who as a body had remained outside the faith'.[20]

What may be said to counteract such impressive judgments? They are probably shared instinctively by most modern liberal readers who surely have little spontaneous sympathy for the quibbles and quarrels of their Roman forbears. The first rejoinder must be simply this: laying aside our own appraisal of these 'fads' and 'taboos', we must first weigh carefully the appraisal given to these matters by the Roman Christians and by the author of the epistle.

As for the Roman brothers, the text makes it clear that the members of Group One viewed the behaviour of Group Two as making them accursed of God. Such sin required their exclusion from fellowship, and strenuous efforts ensued to protect the gospel from this perversion. It is equally clear that members of Group Two viewed members of Group One with scorn, ridicule, and pity, and that they used all kinds of pressures to get them to jettison their 'fads' and 'taboos'. These two groups considered that loyalty to God's saving work in Christ forced them to defend their mutually exclusive positions. Their faith was felt to be dependent on standing by these convictions. To them the point at issue was fundamental; otherwise it would not have been an issue at all.

And what do these chapters reflect concerning Paul's estimate of the issue? They make clear, to be sure, that he had a different idea of what was the point at issue. To him it was not sabbatarianism or vegetarianism. He respected those who in good conscience took opposing positions on those matters. But the point at issue was the daily treatment of opponents by both strong and weak; it was the cumulative and disastrous effect of their quarrels upon the doubters and upon the whole community. It was the demand by each faction that all other believers must live according to its own norm. To Paul this involved an implicit betrayal of the gospel by both factions. This entailed their misunderstanding of the nature of the kingdom of God, along with distorted conceptions of God's justice and mercy. Could anything be more important for Paul than concern about the ruin of men for whom Christ died? Than the threat that 'the offering of the Gentiles' might be unacceptable (15.16)? Than the axioms of ch. 14 which were rejected by the Roman antagonists? Why did Paul spend so much effort in dealing with the trouble-makers if the issue was so ephemeral? Paul was not saying to them: 'a plague on both your houses'; or 'the issue at stake is too trivial for concern'. He was warning them: 'You are both a plague on Christ.' To modern readers the issue may seem unimportant. But no contemporary reader should be encouraged to foist his own hasty appraisals upon the ancient situation.

I believe, then, that there is more than adequate evidence within the chapters themselves to indicate the importance of the issue to Paul and his correspondents. Evidence becomes really overwhelming when we see that Paul viewed the situation in chs. 14 and 15 as the target of the whole epistle. He knew that the difficulty was so deep-seated that it would not yield to pious cliché or emotional appeal. It would yield only to careful, logical argumentation based upon a clear and cogent restatement of the gospel as the power of God for salvation which would make clear what kind of attitudes and actions the obedience of faith demanded. Thus our objective in the analysis which follows is to show how each section of the epistle was oriented towards that target and how, when the reader keeps this target in mind, the earlier steps in Paul's thought become more intelligible and interesting. As K. H. Schelkle has written: 'One would misunderstand Rom. 1–11 if one did not necessarily go on to Rom. 12–15. One would misunderstand 12–15 if the admonitions of these chapters were to hold good without the presupposition of Rom. 1–11.'[21] I would amend that statement only slightly by applying the principle especially to the arguments of 14.1–15.12.

Estimates of importance are highly subjective matters. Readers of the Epistle to the Romans are likely to be too greatly influenced by estimates emanating from either modern theologians or historians. Paul was neither. He wrote this epistle out of his concern for the churches in Rome. His consideration of various theological topics is subordinated to his conviction that 'the process of salvation . . . issues in the reality of the Church . . . as the aim, here and now, of God's plan'.[22] The factions which alienated the congregations were therefore unwitting enemies of God's plan. The importance of that plan required Paul's emphasis in chs. 14, 15 on mutuality, 'the rhythmic sense of reciprocity' to which M. Bouttier calls attention.

The same estimate of importance emerges from reflection upon the centrality of Paul's doctrine of freedom. The strong in faith must have seen themselves as valiant exponents and examples of that doctrine. But the apostle saw in their attitudes a case of total jeopardy for that doctrine. They had been freed. Yes, but this freedom 'dies when it affronts one's brother, weakens a member who is already weak, or leads astray a neighbour who is liable to fall'.[23] To the apostle nothing could be more disastrous than such treasonable examples of Christian liberty. To him, nothing could be more decisive than the issues of chs. 14 and 15.

NOTES

[1] G. O. Griffith, *St. Paul's Gospel to the Romans*, Oxford, 1949, p. 11.

[2] W. Marxsen, *Introduction to the New Testament*, Philadelphia, 1968, pp. 94f. It is through Marxsen that my attention was called to the view of E. Fuchs in *Hermeneutik*, Bad Cannstatt, 1954, p. 191. Of all recent Introductions, that of Marxsen comes closest to my own position. However, I had virtually completed these chapters before I discovered, following the suggestion of John Reumann, the congenial chapter in Marxsen's book.

[3] A. Nygren, *Commentary on Romans*, Philadelphia, 1949; London, 1952.

[4] It is difficult for modern Gentiles, yet necessary, to recall with what horror early Jewish Christians viewed the dangers of eating unclean meat in a Gentile city, cf. E. Haenchen, *Die Apostelgeschichte*, Göttingen, 1956, pp. 418f.

[5] W. D. Davies, *Paul and Rabbinic Judaism*, London, 1955, p. 111.

[6] In the above paragraphs I have drawn upon material from my essay 'The Truth about Sin and Death', in *Interpretation* 7 (1953), pp. 142f.

[7] W. Marxsen, *op. cit.*, pp. 102f.

[8] C. H. Dodd, *Epistle to the Romans*, London and New York, 1932, p. xxviii.

[9] F. J. Leenhardt, *The Epistle to the Romans*, Cleveland and London, 1961, pp. 345f.

[10] 'A definite division may be made between chapters 12 and 13 in which the exhortations are general in character, and 14–15.12 in which they arise directly out of the controversies which are disturbing the Church.' W. Sanday and A. C. Headlam, *The Epistle to the Romans*, Edinburgh and New York, 1902, p. 351. Also W. Marxsen, *op. cit.*, p. 96.

[11] O. Michel, *Der Brief an die Römer*, Göttingen, 1957, p. 341.

[12] W. G. Kümmel, *Introduction to the New Testament*, London and Nashville, 1966, p. 225.

[13] I sometimes suggest to students that they might choose to identify

themselves with one of these people and then write their own autobiography as a visitor to or a member of the Roman congregations, including their own reactions to Paul's letter.

[14] A. Wikenhauser, *New Testament Introduction*, London and New York, 1965, p. 409.

[15] K. Barth, *The Epistle to the Romans*, London, 1933, p. 536.

[16] The reason commonly given for doubting the Pauline authorship of 16.17–20 is the vocabulary. A number of the words are relatively rare in the genuine letters (for a summary, cf. V. Furnish, *Theology and Ethics in Paul*, Nashville, 1968, p. 198). This is a dubious criterion. It assumes that in six or seven authentic letters we have a complete index of Paul's vocabulary. It forgets how often he used words lifted from the vocabulary of his readers. It gives priority to verbal sounds rather than to thought sequences. Paul was far more flexible in his speech patterns than are most Pauline scholars.

[17] R. E. Brown, *The Semitic Background of the Term 'Mystery' in the New Testament*, Philadelphia, 1968, pp. 50–2.

[18] To me the most satisfactory recent treatment of the problems associated with ch. 16 is that found in H. W. Schmidt, *Der Brief des Paulus an die Römer*, Berlin, 1963, pp. 250–67.

[19] C. H. Dodd, *op. cit.*, pp. 214, 219.

[20] A. Wikenhauser, *op. cit.*, p. 407.

[21] K. H. Schelkle, *The Epistle to the Romans*, New York, 1964, p. 193.

[22] M. Bouttier, *Christianity according to Paul* (Studies in Biblical Theology, First Series, 49), 1966, p. 65.

[23] *Ibid.*, p. 111.

II

THE BEGINNING OF THE ARGUMENT: THE FUNCTIONS OF 1.1–17

THE hypothesis with which we begin our review of the earlier sections of the epistle is this: in the last fifth of his letter Paul describes a single complex problem among the Christians in Rome, a situation which he had in mind as he composed the earlier paragraphs of the letter. If this hypothesis is correct, to treat that problem as if it were a trivial matter of fads and prejudices is wholly wrong. Adolf Schlatter is one of the few commentators who realized the importance of this issue:

> Everyone, Paul as well as those in Rome, treats the controversy with the greatest seriousness, because it made apparent a sharp distinction in faith. . . . What made the question so momentous was this: the way in which it was answered was decisive for the entire structuring of the community.[1]

Should either of the extreme positions have become obligatory for all, the community would no longer have been grounded in faith. Hostility had already made it impossible to celebrate the eucharist together. Had it been allowed to destroy the possibility of fellowship among Christians, it would have undermined Paul's apostolic authority and defeated his intention to push towards the far west and to succeed on his hazardous mission to Jerusalem. At stake was the life of all the Gentile churches he had founded, along with their continued acceptance by the Jewish churches. It is not surprising that he should have dealt with this issue with the greatest care, with an argument more subtle and thorough than can be matched elsewhere in his correspondence. Thus far Schlatter.

We now turn to examine the ways in which Paul shaped the opening paragraphs of that argument. Here we call attention to three things: (1) his announcement of his travel plans; (2) his definition of the case which he will argue; (3) his choice of groups to which he will address the different phases of that argument. In each of these areas we discern a similarity between the start and the end of the epistle, a structural symmetry which indicates almost an architectural precision and comprehensiveness on the author's part in giving shape to the letter.

1. We have earlier noted the degree to which the matters mentioned at the outset correspond to those which received attention at the end, showing how the same intentions bracket the intervening chapters. For convenience these may be tabulated:

thanksgiving and commendation	1.8	15.14f.
the centrality of the gospel of God	1.1, 15f.	15.16
Paul's policy in going to new areas	1.13	15.20
his desire to visit Rome	1.10	15.23
the frustration of that desire	1.13	15.22
his assignment to Gentiles	1.5	15.15f.
the mutuality of indebtedness	1.12, 14	15.27
his wish to strengthen their faith	1.11	15.13; 16.25

All of the items above have a bearing upon Paul's purposes in writing this letter.

2. Now we may notice ways in which Paul began to define the case which he would argue, and which, if successful, would make cogent the position which he took at the end (chs. 14, 15). In this connection a glance at the salutation is necessary. In comparison with the salutations in other letters, this is the longest and the most complex. The beginning and end are typical but what comes between is not.

. . . set apart for the gospel of God which he promised beforehand through his prophets in the holy scriptures, the gospel concerning his Son, who was descended from David according to the flesh and designated Son of God in power according to the Spirit of holiness by his resurrection from the dead, Jesus Christ our Lord, through whom we received grace and apostleship to bring about the obedience of faith for the sake of his name among all the nations [Gentiles], including yourselves who are called to belong to Jesus Christ (1.2–6).

Why should Paul thus change the conventional form? Why so laboured a description of the gospel? I venture to suggest that the reasons are the same as those which prompted the christological references in 15.1–21. At the outset the writer is appealing tacitly to the members of Groups One and Two, reminding them how the gospel of God had destroyed their extreme positions by its inclusion of both Jews and Gentiles. On the one hand, what had happened had happened in fulfilment of the 'promises given to the patriarchs' (15.8), the promises 'through his prophets in the holy scriptures' (1.2). It had been essential for Christ to become a servant to circumcised (15.8) and to be 'descended from David according to the flesh' (1.3). On the other hand, God had not limited his gospel to the Jews. God had enabled the Gentiles to glorify God for his mercy (15.9), thus uniting them with Israel. This miracle had been made possible by the designation of Jesus as Son of God by his resurrection from the dead (1.4), so that the Gentiles might be saved (1.5) and called to be saints with the Jews (the *all* of 1.7).[2] In this deft way Paul called the weak in faith to recognize that there would have been no gospel at all apart from God's welcome of Gentiles through his powerful act in the resurrection. Yet he also reminded the strong in faith to give full weight to the fact of Jesus' sonship to David in fulfilment of the scriptures. The interdependence of Jews and Gentiles was thus declared to be integral to God's plan, to the ministry (διακονία) of Christ to the circumcised (15.8), to the resurrection of Christ from the dead (1.4), to Paul's vocation as slave (δοῦλος) of Christ and apostle (1.5; 15.16), and to all who are called to be saints (1.7). Accordingly, those who prided themselves on the strength of their faith must accept that definition of strength which had been embodied in the resurrection. (The use of the word δύναμις [strength, power] in this connection is a significant link to the strong [οἱ δυνατοί] of ch. 14.) They must not despise those in the lineage of David who still obeyed the scriptures. The latter in turn must not condemn those whom God had not condemned, that is, the Gentiles whom God had welcomed in the resurrection and to whom God had commissioned the apostle (1.4f.). All whom God had 'called to belong to Jesus Christ' must be respected because their faith represented a fulfilment of scripture and not its erasure. All were called to the same life of holiness, a life empowered by the same divine Spirit and expressed by a welcome as inclusive as God's. Each group was deeply indebted to the other group.[3]

It is altogether likely that in the development of the dissensions in Rome, the position of Paul had already served as a source of friction, accentuating the existing animosities (cf. 9.1; 10.1f.). To members of Group One he had probably become known as destroyer of the Law and defender of unrestricted licence. Members of Group Two may well have suspected him as a Jew of undue loyalty to his kinsmen. It had been rumoured that in other churches he repressed liberty for the sake of expediency. He may thus have been damned by both extremes, but for opposite reasons. They would have been inclined, before receiving his letter, to discount his arguments. How could he, then, disarm both sets of enemies? For one thing, he announced himself as slave of Christ. That would establish common ground with them all. Yet he openly affirmed his assignment as apostle to all the Gentiles. No hint of a compromise there. He had been sent to Gentiles, however, 'to bring about the *obedience* of faith' and not simply to proclaim and to defend their emancipation (cf. 15.15f.). Even though he was primarily responsible for the Gentile mission, he confessed his indebtedness to all, he sent 'grace and peace' to all, he recognized that all are 'beloved' of God (1.7). Thus he avoided a total identification with either Group One or Two, and he established a common ground with both, so that each might be willing to listen to his later arguments.

Even though Paul thus used a long salutation to advance his cause, the first precise definition of his case comes in the famous verses 1.16f. I believe that in writing these verses Paul also was keenly aware of the antagonisms with which he would openly deal in ch. 14.

For I am not ashamed of the gospel: it is the power of God for salvation to every one who has faith, to the Jew first and also to the Greek. For in it the righteousness of God is revealed through faith for faith; as it is written, 'He who through faith is righteous shall live' (1.16f.).

The lowly conjunction *for* should not be overlooked. It links these verses to the preceding statements in which the apostle presented his hopes in sending the letter and in planning the projected visit to Rome. In fact, the punctuation is here an element in interpretation. What if there were a comma and not a period after v. 15? We would be reminded more forcefully that the theological argument which follows is occasioned by the apostolic intention which precedes, an intention shaped by the situations described in ch. 14.

Notice how specific and germane this statement becomes when interpreted in the light of those situations. Who could be said to be ashamed of the gospel? Were they ashamed because it lacked power? When they condemned members of Group Two, the weak in faith were ashamed of the gospel because they believed it was impotent to turn Gentiles away from their sins. In ridiculing members of Group One, the strong were denying that the gospel had sufficient power to free the scrupulous from reliance upon their taboos. Paul was not ashamed, as others were; to him the gospel had *power* to save *everyone* who had *faith*.[4] Notice how Paul adopted here the very words which were used in the slogans and shibboleths of the strong in faith. The term translated power (δύναμις) was cognate to the terms strong and weak (δυνατοί versus ἀδύνατοι). Inherent in these epithets was a basic corruption of the concept of the strength of the gospel. Partisans had been measuring the strength of men, not the power of God. According to Paul, such power must be redefined by the lordship of Christ, by his resurrection as God's Son, by the sanctifying Spirit (1.4). It can be received and perceived only as *God's* power, a power designed to save men. The partisans bickered over the degrees of power. They did not deny faith. Even the invidious insult 'weak in faith' implied the existence of faith. Paul rejected the assumptions of both, however, when he asserted that everyone who has faith (whether strong or weak) has received God's power for salvation. By redefining the concept of strength or power, Paul celebrated the bridging of the greatest chasm in human society, the chasm between Jew and Greek. But members of Groups One and Two were in effect refusing to use that bridge. They had not allowed the gospel to redefine their own estimates of what constituted weakness and strength.

Another term had become polluted in their partisan wrangling: faith. The strong used it as a basis for self-righteousness and boasting; their adversaries measured its existence by observance of diets and days. Each group assumed that it could measure the other's faith, and each was forced by that measurement to refuse to associate with the other. They denied Paul's premiss that faith is a matter solely between a man and God (14.22) and therefore a matter not open to social judgment (14.10). But Paul insisted that God alone knows the degree of faith, inasmuch as it is he who gives faith through the gospel to every believer. Here, as everywhere in the letter, Paul repudiated the understanding of faith which was held by the partisans. Yet his conception of faith was such as to establish common ground with the whole range of believers, from the most scrupulous Jew to the most emancipated Gentile. At the outset he announced his determination to construct his argument on that foundation. He was thankful for faith's presence in the Roman brothers (1.8). He viewed his whole task as an apostle as being designed to produce the obedience of faith (1.5). Therefore he wished to strengthen their faith (1.12). This constellation of convictions is repeated in ch. 14, where God's power is also set over against the prejudices of the antagonists (14.4, 7–9), and where salvation was assured to everyone who had faith, to all who gave thanks to God, who honoured the Lord, whose death and resurrection had (as in 1.3–5) given him power over the dead and the living, over all who 'belong to him' (cf. 1.6 and 14.8).

Many scholars treat 1.16 as the theme which embraces all that Paul would write in the first eleven chapters. So it is. But if this verse is the Alpha of the argument, the Omega may be found in the axioms of ch. 14. This beginning and this end form the brackets within which the course of the discussion emerges.

The argument may become even clearer when one studies the correspondences between 1.17 and ch. 14. For one thing, there are subtle links with 14.23 which the usual English translation obscures.

He who has doubts is condemned, if he eats, because he does not act from faith (ἐκ πίστεως); for whatever does not proceed from faith (ἐκ πίστεως) is sin (14.23).

For in it [the gospel] the righteousness of God is revealed through faith for faith (ἐκ πίστεως εἰς πίστιν): as it is written, 'He who through faith (ἐκ πίστεως) is righteous shall live' (1.17).

The translation of these phrases into English is as strategic as it is difficult. One might say that all the verses in which the phrase 'from faith' appears are pivotal to Paul's thinking. In three key passages, the phrase appears twice (4.16 in addition to the two above. Cf. below, p. 55).

In all three, Paul was dealing with believers, with those who have faith. In all, the issue was the correct understanding of what proceeds from or does not proceed from their faith. Faith was viewed as a source, a taproot, a seed, an originating ground. But of what? To that question Paul and the partisans of Rome gave different answers. 1.17 indicates that life, righteousness and salvation proceed from faith. 14.23 indicates that everything not so proceeding is sin. An action generated from doubt is sin. To condemn or to despise a brother is sin. To deny God the power to judge and to save a brother is sin. So faith yields righteousness, not sin. But is not this a surrender to the perspective of the weak in faith? Not at all. It simply shifts the point at issue from the observance of rules to the definition of righteousness and to the selection of yardsticks for measuring it. This is the question which Paul takes up immediately (1.18ff.) as providing the substance of debate with Groups One and Two.

We must return now to a single phrase: 'from faith to faith'. What does that mean? Interpreters have varied widely in their definitions. (1) 'From the faith of a preacher to the faith of a listener' – perhaps in line with 1.12, 15; (2) 'from the faithfulness of God to the responding faith of the believer'; (3) a way of stressing the truth that righteousness is exclusively God's gift and is communicated *by faith alone*; (4) 'from faith inherited to faith newly received'; (5) 'from implicit to explicit faith' in the life of each believer; (6) the phrase stresses continual progress in faith, since faith is both the ground and the goal of the believer's existence.

I believe that here again there is a polemic edge in Paul's formulation. The righteousness of God is revealed as proceeding out of faith (the opposite of sin) in the direction of a stronger faith. Everything which proceeds from faith tends to produce a greater or stronger faith. Such is in fact the test of what does proceed from faith. This criterion is contrary to that adopted by Groups One and Two in Rome; it suggests a quite different orientation. To a degree, it supports the basic contention of Group Two, but it destroys their rejection of Group One and sets a different goal for their own development. This understanding is very similar to that of O. Michel who suggests that the phrase may be an abbreviation for the phrase 'from the obedience of faith toward the obedience of faith'.[5] It was such progression which Paul believed was being denied by the partisans in Rome. A long and cogent debate would be required to convince them of it, and in the end the apostle can only pray that God will himself produce that obedience (16.26). Although this interpretation of the phrase remains uncertain, there is no uncertainty about the fact that the whole epistle deals with false and true ideas of the style of life which proceeds from faith (1.17). These verses, I believe, announce the case to be argued, and chs. 14 and 15 clinch the bearing of that argument upon the house-churches in Rome.[6]

3. Let us now appraise the value of this section of the letter (1.1–17) in clarifying the question of which groups in Rome Paul was addressing. Every good 'Introduction to the New Testament' sets forth an answer to the question: whom was Paul addressing in Rome? That question quickly becomes: was he writing to Jewish or to Gentile Christians? With the field tacitly limited to two answers, many scholars take the first option. Others, for whom W. G. Kümmel is an able exponent, take the second:

> The Epistle unambiguously designates its readers as Gentile Christians (1.5, 13; 11.13; 15.15f.). . . . Any attempt to obtain a picture of the readers of Romans must proceed from this fixed point.[7]

But can the options be so easily reduced to two? Kümmel himself is forced to recognize that the Roman congregation was not purely Gentile in its makeup. He admits that the appeal to the strong and the weak for mutual acceptance 'would be pointless if both groups were not presupposed in the congregation' (15.7f.). Kümmel's dilemma would be lessened if he were to admit the existence in Rome of many house-churches rather than assuming only a single congregation. We have detected in chs. 14–16 evidence not only for the separate existence of several hostile congregations but also for at least five different factions with whom Paul would have to deal in writing a circular letter which Phoebe would deliver to them all. Moreover, it is not likely that these factions could be simply identified by the terms Jew and Gentile (witness the examples of Paul, Prisca and Aquila, Epaenetus, etc.). I believe that Paul recognized the existence of this pluralism before he began to write his salutation to his readers.

He distinguished God's treatment of Jew and Greek (1.16; 15.8; 16.26) in each case mentioning the Jew first, presumably for polemical as well as for historical and theological reasons. He addressed the scattered congregations in such a way as to affirm his own role among the Gentiles, yet in such a way as to express the indebtedness of Gentile Christians to Jews, and his own indebtedness as a Jew to the Gentiles, whether wise or foolish (1.14). Although he addressed the Gentile Christians in Rome as distinguished from Jewish believers, he immediately saluted 'all God's beloved', and thus intimated that he expected his letter to be read in some congregations which were Gentile, in some which were Jewish, and in some where both would be present. It is to be expected therefore that in various sections of his letter the apostle would have one of these three types of congregations especially in mind. If in each successive paragraph the identity of this group of readers can be determined, the reader's understanding of Paul's ideas will be enhanced. This is not always possible, for at times the apostle shifts from one audience to another very quickly and without clear signals. 1.6, for example, illustrates an address to the Gentiles; in 1.7 he addresses all. In 1.8 he begins a paragraph with the more inclusive 'all of you' but ends by speaking in a more limited fashion of 'you' as set over against 'the *rest* of the Gentiles'. Then, in 1.16f. he sets forth a theme applicable equally to all participants in the dialogue, but immediately begins a long discussion which appears to be oriented primarily towards a Jewish-Christian audience (2.1f.).

Precisely this same kind of shift characterizes the last three chapters. For example, 14.1 is addressed to the strong; 14.3b, 4 are addressed to the weak; 15.7 is addressed to both. Moreover, the address to these three audiences includes, as do 1.1–17, a corresponding discussion of God's dealings with Jews, with Gentiles, and with both included within a single worshipping community. From the beginning to the end, the reader is led to suppose that a paragraph intended primarily for Jewish Christians will be overheard by Gentile Christians, and vice versa.[8] Only an apostle who was adept in dealing with many factions could orient his argument in such a way as to be effective with each separately and with all collectively. And to do that he must use and redefine the words which were essential but the differing meanings of which were involved in the confrontations: faith, righteousness, sin, law, Jew, Gentile, salvation, life, gospel, death, resurrection, grace, and obedience. The understanding of these terms was decisive in chs. 1 and 14; it also determined the flow of the arguments in the sections between.

NOTES

[1] A. Schlatter, *Gottes Gerechtigkeit*, Stuttgart, 1952, pp. 363f.

[2] F. C. Porter was quite right in defining the christological significance of this reference to the resurrection. 'This new sense in which Jesus became Son of God . . . is not a sense that separates him from men after he had been united with them on earth; on the contrary it is a sense that unites him with men more closely than before.' (*The Mind of Christ in Paul*, New York and London, 1930. p. 266.) I would add only that there is a quite special sense in which his birth as Son of David united Jesus to Jews and in which his resurrection as Son of God united him to Gentiles. I believe that Paul was making this special point in his expansion of the usual epistolary salutation.

[3] At this point I urge readers to study Appendix 2. The power of gratitude, whether in the apostolic work of Paul or in the healing of schisms like those in Rome, is usually neglected.

[4] It is easy to suppose that the word *all* appears so frequently in Romans (more than seventy times) because of Paul's rhetorical penchant for euphemism and hyperbole. Rather it carries a strong polemical thrust. He was fighting with his partisan readers and trying to persuade them to draw a much wider circle in their conception of the boundaries of the community of faith. As Paul saw it, that community embraced the two most hostile factions. Cf. W. Marxsen, *op. cit.* p. 102.

[5] O. Michel, *op. cit.*, p. 45.

[6] Because our stereotypes of Paul so frequently reflect modern ideas of what faith is and what it means to be a missionary and an apostle, every reader needs to divest himself of those stereotypes in so far as he can so that he can visualize the original situation more accurately. Perhaps Appendix 1 may offer help in this regard.

[7] W. G. Kümmel, *op. cit.*, p. 219.

[8] In some sections of his argument, Paul consciously addresses all factions, but in others he concentrates upon dealing with the position of a particular faction. In order that readers may see at a glance my division of the epistle, I indicate it here.

Section	Primary audience for Paul's arguments
1.1–17	All readers, but with distinctions recognized
1.18–4.15	Group One
4.16–5.21	All readers, with distinctions recognized
6.1–23	Group Two
7.1–8.8	Group One
8.9–11.12	Group Three
11.13–13.14	Group Two
14.1–15.32	Alternating address to Groups One, Two, Three
16.1–27	All readers

III

'THERE IS NO DISTINCTION': THE LOGIC OF 1.18–4.25

OUR first task is to determine to which group in the Roman churches Paul was speaking in this section. The answer in brief is this: at the beginning he addressed the weak in faith; at the end (4.16f.) he moved to include all Roman Christians. So limited an address may be challenged. Leenhardt, for example, thinks that here 'Paul addresses himself to a fictitious opponent'.[1] This concept appears to be supported by the fact that the style of these paragraphs is so similar to that of diatribe, which was a highly popular form of writing in the first century among teachers and preachers.

It often becomes easier to follow Paul's arguments if the reader imagines the apostle face to face with a heckler, who makes interjections and receives replies which sometimes are withering or brusque.[2]

My conviction is, on the contrary, that the 'you' which is so prominent in 2.1–6 and 2.17–24 applies more precisely to one of the factions in Rome. The behaviour which Paul singles out for special attention is that of judging and condemning others. The key word is κρίνω which appears ten times here (2.1, 3, 12, 16, 27; 3.4, 6, 7). It appears nowhere else in Romans except in ch. 14 (vv. 3, 4, 5, 10, 13, 22) where it is essential to the description of Group One. We have already noted that Paul considered the sin of this faction as lying not in vegetarianism or sabbatarianism but in the condemnatory attitude towards Christian brothers. The same judgmental stance is attacked by the apostle in chs. 2 and 3. It is in their judging others, secure in their own self-righteousness, that they draw upon themselves God's condemnation. In these opening chapters Paul began to construct his case against them. To that case we shall return in a moment.

First it is important to see in what detail Paul describes this

partisan group. In ch. 14 the terms used were those adopted by
their enemies; we do not learn how they thought of themselves. In
2.17f., however, Paul lets us look in their mirror. Here he, like
their opponents, inevitably distorts the image. These are the key
items in their self-image: they call themselves Jews; they have
been instructed in the Law and they rely on it; they worship God,
know his will, and are proud of their status as his people; they
believe that God has made them teachers and guides, wise
counsellors to the foolish, and has given them in the Law 'the
embodiment of knowledge and truth'. It is because of this picture
of themselves that in the name of the Law they condemn Gentiles
as thieves, adulterers, and idolators. They are convinced of their
own circumcision (2.25) and of its value (3.1), and they therefore
believe that they are better off (3.9) than their Gentile brothers.
Probably the sombre list of Gentile sins which Paul gave in 1.18–32
is one which they enjoyed citing. The apostle indicated his kinship
with them not only in deploring that dark display of Gentile
derelictions, but more directly in his use of first person pronouns.
Thus 'their faithlessness' in 3.3 becomes 'our wickedness' in 3.5.
His attack upon their proud claims led to the question: 'Are *we*
Jews any better off?' (3.9). And since these claims were based on
the claim of descent from Abraham, Paul spoke twice of '*our*
father Abraham' (4.1, 12). One can be quite confident, therefore,
that in this whole section of the epistle the author was speaking
directly to the Jewish spokesmen of the weak in faith and that
these paragraphs give a polemical portrait of their position.

That position was one in which self-approval was at every point
expressed by attacks on others. The apostle was therefore impelled
to deal with their basic attitudes towards both Gentiles and Jews.
He was addressing members of Group One, but since his target
was their self-righteous condemnation of the strong in faith, Paul
found it necessary to deal first with the status of all Gentiles.
Although their immediate animosity was directed against Gentile
Christians, that animosity was a carry-over from their earlier
attitudes towards all Gentiles. Thus Paul was forced to deal with
the larger group (1.18–32) before taking up the position of Christian Gentiles (2.14–16, 26, 29). His immediate objective was to
prove that God had changed the criteria of measurement. Members
of Group One had assumed, both before and after their own
conversion, that the major distinction between human communities

must continue to be that between Jew and Gentile. To Paul this conception of things had been totally abrogated by God's action in Christ: 'There is no distinction.' The only distinction which survived the resurrection of Jesus was the distinction between faith and unbelief, and within the Christian fellowship the only important distinction between what does not proceed from faith (14.23) and what does so proceed (1.16f.).

Looking now at the colourful appraisal of the Gentile world in 1.18–32, we should ask what function that paragraph played in Paul's argument with leaders of Group One. Speaking generally, we can say that Paul was laying an ambush for them by painting a portrait with which they would eagerly agree. Once they had marched into the trap, he would close the exits. He used the form and vocabulary of traditional attacks on idolatry with which they were familiar (e.g. Wisdom of Solomon 13.6–9; 14.22). His catalogue of vices were those which spokesmen of the synagogues had long employed. The very sins which these spokesmen were commissioned by the Law to resist – theft, adultery, idolatry (2.21–23) – were fully exemplified by the Gentile world. The apostle agreed with them on the fatal character of such sins. Gentiles had enjoyed ample opportunity to know God but they had suppressed this knowledge. In other words, he was conceding to his adversaries a basic justification for their rejection of fellowship with Gentiles.

Yet this concession was also a debater's trick, for he immediately used this apparent agreement to disarm them. Notice three things. First, the coincidence of the phrase 'without excuse' in 1.20 and 2.1. These are the only occurrences of this Greek word in the New Testament. They are quite intentionally balanced here:

'*They* [the Gentiles] are without excuse.'
'*You* [Jewish–Christian judges] are without excuse.'

What were the reasons for this second accusation? The Jewish–Christian judges had no excuse, for in judging others they condemned themselves. In their judgment of others (and this is something of which the weak in faith would require proof) they were doing the same things. Could Paul substantiate this charge? His whole case depended on it. He could sustain it only by a different analysis of the root sin of the judged Gentiles and only by convincing the Jewish–Christian judges of the validity of that analysis.

The second thing to notice, therefore, is Paul's analysis of what was the root sin of the Gentiles. Not the lusts of 1.24, or the dishonourable passions of 1.26, or the evils of 1.29. Those were things to which God 'gave them up' as penalties for a deeper and earlier betrayal. The source of such wickedness was an inward Godward attitude described in threefold fashion:

> They did not honour (δοξάζω) him as God. . . .
> They did not give thanks to him (εὐχαριστῶ). . . .
> They claimed to be wise. . . .

This leads us to a third noteworthy feature. These accusations correspond in a reverse way to Paul's description of two major factions in Rome. Both the strong and the weak there do give thanks to God (εὐχαριστῶ, 14.6); and this act of gratitude is far more decisive in God's eyes than their dietary practices (although they did not grant this).[3] Both follow their diverse practices 'in honour of the Lord', to whom they live and die. Paul viewed this common participation in glorifying God as an ultimate goal (15.6–9). In other words, the Gentiles whose behaviour and fate are described in 1.18–32 were to be sharply distinguished from the strong in faith (Gentile Christians) whose behaviour is described in 14.1–9. The weak in faith often failed to make that distinction, but rather identified the two groups of Gentiles as grounds for their condemnation of lawless Christians.

It was this root sin which entitled Paul, on the other hand, to apply the accusations against the Gentiles (in 1.18–32) to the Jewish–Christian judges in 2.1–24. Because the sins were the same, the God who shows 'no partiality' would visit both groups with 'tribulation and distress' (2.9).

They did not honour God as God but rather stole from him the right to judge (2.1–3). They did not give thanks to him but rather presumed upon his kindness and forbearance (2.4). According to this way of reasoning, thanksgiving and pride are mutually exclusive. One cannot simultaneously judge others and be thankful to God. Thanksgiving to God for the gospel is designed to consort with penitence, not self-righteousness. In the act of judging they had refused such gratitude; they had substituted a sense of their own achievement for the patience required by God. Their very factiousness (ἐριθεία covers exactly the kind of jealous wrangling found in the Roman congregations) proved that they were disobedient to that very special truth of God which had been revealed in the gospel of Christ (15.8). It is no accident that in 2.8 the Jewish judges are accused of the very same substitution of ἀδικία (unrighteousness) for ἀλήθεια (truth) which in 1.18 is the charge against their Gentile convicts. The visible form of their external behaviour was doubtless very different, but judged by the internal source the sin was identical.

Both the Gentile sinners and Jewish judges claimed to be wise (1.22, 2.17–20). It was this very claim that marked sermons against stealing as theft from God. The condemnation of adultery, since it replaced penitent thanksgiving, made them adulterers. It was their pride in the Law which induced them to break the law, to dishonour God, and to blaspheme his name among the Gentiles. Here is strong language, but such language was required to break the deceptive chains of self-congratulation. To the weak in faith who condemned the liberties of the strong, Paul was saying: 'If you call Gentile Christians blasphemous idolators, these brothers who give thanks to God, you make yourselves guilty of that very sin.'

This cannot mean that the critic also practices homosexual perversions and the like. . . . Paul's point is that in the very act of judging the judge is involved in the same conduct as the man he condemns. Behind all the sins of 1.29ff. lies the sin of idolatry which reveals man's ambition to put himself in the place of God and so to be his own Lord. But this is precisely what the judge does.[4]

Moreover, this idolatry affects others besides the Christian Jew. It leads to blasphemy when he persuades the Gentile Christian to share the same devotion to a false God (2.24).

This view of Paul's rationale in using 1.18–32 as the basis for his sharp attack on Group One in the Roman church may serve to explain one feature of 1.32 which has puzzled exegetes: 'They not only do them but also approve those who practise them.' Barrett defines the puzzle thus: 'The words "not only . . . but also" suggest an increase in the offence; but to approve of those who sin can scarcely be regarded as worse than sinning.'[5] If we are right in our understanding of Paul's debate with Group One (2.1 – those who do not approve) as requiring this concession, this ambush by means of a gloomy portrait of the Gentile world, we should ask why the strong in faith (Group Two) are nowhere mentioned, since the difficulty in Rome involved them, and they are excluded from this portrait by 1.18–23. One answer is 1.32b. The leaders of Group One may have accused the leaders of Group Two not of doing these 'sins' but of 'approval' of their Gentile kinsmen who do them.

Whether or not this explanation has merit, I hope the main point is clear. In what he says about the sins of Gentiles, Paul is more concerned with factiousness in Rome than with general views of Gentile depravity. This is why in ch. 2 he tried first to prove to Jewish Christians that their prideful condemnations of Gentile culture placed them on the same level in God's eyes and subject to the same penalties as the Gentiles. In fact, although God shows no partiality, the Jew is given priority in receiving God's wrath – 'the Jew first and also the Greek' (2.10). Yet the apostle's attention primarily focused on the relations of Jewish critic to Gentile Christians, that is, to those who have in fact chosen to give honour and gratitude to God and who do not claim to be wise. 'Look,' he said to his Jewish–Christian brothers, 'it is not only that your sin in condemning the strong in faith puts you on the same level with the Gentiles whom you detest; it is also that the faith-based righteousness of your Gentile–Christian brothers puts them on the same level with you.'

This, I believe, is the function of 2.12–16, 25–29 in the argument. Gentile *believers*, although they did not possess the Law, were doing by nature what the Law required. Their hearts and consciences bore witness to the existence of a genuine covenant with God. Because they kept the precepts of the Law in this sense, their uncircumcision must be regarded as circumcision (2.26). Inwardly they were authentic Jews, spiritually circumcised, receiving God's praise for their circumcised hearts. As such, they had turned the tables on their judges. By receiving God's welcome (15.7) and his praise (2.29), they were now in the position of condemning the weak in faith, whose external and physical circumcision and whose possession of the Law had been betrayed in their self-righteousness. Nothing in any of Paul's letters, not even the stinging attack of Rom. 16.17–20, is more brutally sharp than this direct charge against the members of Group One, that by condemning the members of Group Two they were equally sinful with the Gentile world and were actually inferior to the Christian brothers whose faith they denied. Brutally sharp, yes. But an effective therapy for a disease as subtle as this required bitter medicine.

So bitter was the medicine that Paul immediately raises a point which they were bound to present in rebuttal. If what Paul had written was true, they would be sure to accuse Paul of teaching that the Jew had no advantage, and circumcision had no value (3.1). Such a position seemed to force upon all Christians the radical antinomianism of Group Two. The details of Paul's treatment of this protest in 3.1 will be passed over, inasmuch as we are here concerned only with his dialogue with members of Group One. We have already concluded that in this chapter, as in ch. 14, the basic fault of members of this Group was their arrogation to themselves of the right to condemn others (2.1). It was this which constituted blasphemy and the breaking of the Law (2.24). Their questions (3.1) were answered in terms of this situation. On the one hand, so long as they are under the power of sin (whatever does not proceed from faith) they are no better off than Gentiles. It is to them as sinners that the Law speaks (3.19). They will be judged by the very God whose power to judge they have tried to steal from him. The selection of citations from the Psalms and Isaiah to apply to them was especially appropriate, for they thought of themselves as guides to the blind (2.19).

On the other hand, Paul did not deny all advantages to the Jews. They had received a special trust from God – the scriptures. But the very purpose of these oracles had been to serve as witness to God's faithfulness. Those who used them for their own advantage were rightly condemned as sinners. So long as the process of judging others continued, the weak in faith stood condemned by the Law which they served. The function of the Law was not to support their claim to superiority but to convey knowledge of their own sin against their fellows. It established the fact that among sinners there is no distinction (2.1–11).

This same fact is established through faith in Jesus Christ – 'there is no distinction' among believers (e.g. between members of Groups One and Two). To be sure, Paul concedes to believing Jews the undeniable importance of the Law and the Prophets. Yet this concession is found in the same sentence in which he declares that God's righteousness has been manifested apart from law (3.21). Here again it is clear that Paul is speaking primarily to Jewish believers about their attitude towards Gentile believers who do not accept the Law. Yet he speaks to one group about another group in such a way as to destroy any distinction between them. Or rather, he points to the fact that sin had destroyed that distinction and that God had made its restoration impossible by making his righteousness accessible to all 'by his grace as a gift'. The circumcised and the uncircumcised had been united by sinning; they were now united by believing. The oneness of God was thus demonstrated by the results of his divine forbearance for all (3.30). Members of Group One were thus declared to be denying the oneness of God both by condemning sinful Gentiles and by boasting of their superiority in possessing and obeying the Law.

Again, however, they raised protests. They were not ready to concede so easy a victory to this protagonist of Gentile believers, this enemy of the Law. They tried to shift the basis of argument from their own actions to the objective existence of the Law and of their forefather Abraham. They accused Paul and his supporters of using faith to overthrow the Law (3.31) and of denying to Abraham and his lineage any unique place in the divine plan (4.1). The reply of the apostle was designed to focus upon the specific faults of his opponents and to separate Abraham from those faults. (1) 'Our forefather,' he writes in effect, 'did not use his special position as an occasion for boasting before God, as you do.' (2) 'He did not, like you, view obedience to the Law as a means of meriting special blessings from God.' (3) 'In his case it was not circumcision which distinguished him from the uncircumcised, but faith which distinguished him from unbelievers. For this reason he became the father of all who believe; there is no distinction among them.' It could not be clearer that Paul was declaring to the weak in faith: 'You must accept the strong in faith as children of Abraham and heirs to the promise of Abraham.' 'Our' father (4.1) has become the father of 'us all' (4.16). If you do not accept this, then faith is null and the promise is void (4.14).

In the last paragraph of ch. 4, where he had arrived at the assertion of Abraham's common paternity of Gentile and Jewish believers, the apostle began to speak directly to all members of the Roman churches. Since they were all Abraham's children, without distinction, the apostle now presented Abraham's faith as an example for them all. In this presentation we detect ample evidence that the writer kept at the centre of his concern the animosities noted in ch. 14. Let us review this evidence. There are at least six distinct links between this paragraph and the situation described in chs. 14 and 15.

Paul took good care to dissociate Abraham from the weak in faith, using precisely the same phrase in this connection, 'he did not become weak in faith'. This was a direct attack upon those who appealed to their descent from Abraham as giving them priority in God's eyes. While recognizing such descent 'according to the flesh' (4.1), the apostle viewed Abraham's attitude towards his own body as the antithesis of confidence in such descent. In claiming such superiority, members of Group One in fact disproved any kinship to Abraham through faith.

2. The apostle explicitly asserted that Abraham did not belong to Group Three, the doubters. Here again the same phrase was utilized. 'No distrust made him waver concerning the promise of God.' The phrase 'he did not doubt' (οὐ διεκρίθη) is the opposite of 'he who has doubts' (διακρινόμενος) in 14.23. In both cases such wavering is viewed as ἀπιστία, the absence of faith. Abraham had every reason to waver, and did not. The members of Group Three had every reason not to waver, and did. The difference lay in the degree of confidence in God's power to fulfil his promise to the fathers (15.8).

3. Not content with this explicit use of two partisan labels, Paul used still a third to associate Abraham directly with Group Five. 'He grew strong in his faith' (4.20 ἐνεδυναμώθη τῇ πίστει). We have seen that the measurement of the strength of faith was a central point at issue in community relationships in Rome. Here the apostle used the example of Abraham to settle the issue. In so doing, of course, he dissociated the patriarch sharply from the position of those who self-confidently claimed to be strong (Group Two). The strength of Abraham's faith did not lie in his views of holy days and of clean foods or in his tendency to despise other believers. Rather it consisted in his readiness to give glory to God. Such glory expressed the fact that he was fully convinced in his own mind (14.5 and 4.21 are the only two passages in Romans where πληροφορέω was used). This conviction expressed his readiness to believe against hope in God's power to 'call into existence the things that do not exist'. In 4.21 the apostle decisively located strength not in man but in God (only God is δυνατός), and thereby traced the process by which Abraham grew stronger to his faith-relationship to God.

4. The accent on Abraham as 'the father of *many nations*' (4.17) paralleled the picture in ch. 15 of the intention of God to include Jews and Gentiles within a single worshipping community, a community joyful and at peace, a community where Christ's welcome of all had become the measure of Jewish and Gentile welcome of each other. Faith in God must accordingly be translated immediately into such unreserved welcome. This thrust of both passages constituted the apostle's strong support of Groups Four and Five, those who gave full weight to the discovery that Abraham 'is the father of us all' (4.16) and to the corollary that all are therefore called upon to 'glorify God for his mercy' (15.9).

5. Although faith makes all believers sons of Abraham because of its common radicality, the faith of Abraham was occasioned by one event (the promise as expressed in Gen. 17.5; Rom. 4.17) whereas the faith of the Roman Christians was occasioned by another (the death and resurrection of Jesus [4.24f.]). The apostle's argument rested upon the comparability of God's promises and God's actions in these two events and upon the resulting correspondence in the character of faith. This position was bound to collide with the convictions of Group One, whose members gave priority to God's action in Abraham, which appeared to them to place a premium upon that righteousness which comes through works and through circumcision (4.1–12). It was bound to collide also with the position of Group Two for whom the work of Christ nullified the promise to Abraham and justified them in despising Abraham's descendants. For Paul, however, faith in the gospel of Jesus was identical with the faith of Abraham and conferred sonship to him (4.24f.). The righteousness which proceeded from the faith (ἐκ πίστεως) of Abraham was identical with the righteousness which proceeded from the faith (ἐκ πίστεως) of his descendants (4.16, cf. above, p. 41). A comparison between 14.7–9 and 4.24f. should make this clear. The central result of the death and resurrection of Jesus was his lordship over them. They henceforth gave thanks to God, glorified him in all situations, and lived or died to him alone. That had been the basic pattern of Abraham's dependence on God.

6. Involved in the other links between the two passages is a similar emphasis on a view of faith as hoping against hope in the power of God to fulfil his promise. As Paul analysed the situation in Rome, he saw that what was needed by all factions was such a

hope (15.12f.). In condemning their licentious brethren, the weak in faith were in fact denying the Lord's power to make them stand (14.4). In despising their scrupulous brethren, the strong were in fact guilty of the same hopelessness. Both were making a man's faith subject to another man's measurement and thereby denying the power of God's grace. Neither was fully convinced that God was able to do what he had promised. They were living from the past rather than the future, from mundane estimates of possibilities rather than from faith's reliance on God's power to raise the dead (4.17, 25; 14.9). Strong faith is grounded in an ontological revolution, in which the recognition of God's presence releases his power to transform death into life whenever Abraham and his sons risk everything in hoping for that life.

To sum up, there is an amazing degree of continuity between this picture of Abraham and the axioms of Paul's position in chs 14 and 15. Such continuity is far from accidental. If the apostle could convince the members of Groups One, Two and Three that faith in God's gospel had cancelled out the former distinctions among them, virtually all his other objectives in the letter would come within his reach.

NOTES

[1] F. J. Leenhardt, *op. cit.*, p. 75.
[2] C. K. Barrett, *Epistle to the Romans*, London and New York, 1957, p. 43.
[3] Appendix 2.
[4] C. K. Barrett, *op. cit.*, pp. 43f.
[5] *Ibid.*, p. 41.

IV

'LIFE FOR ALL MEN': THE DIALECTIC
OF 5.1–8.39

THE Epistle to the Romans has invited a vast variety of interpretations. So diverse are these interpretations that it is easy to claim too little for any single interpretation or, on the other hand, to claim too much. The latter is the immediate danger in this current study. To offset this danger, let me urge the reader to remember that in setting forth certain specific purposes of the apostle it is not our intention to restrict Paul's concerns within a narrow orbit, but rather to notice how his wide-ranging thought came to a focus upon definite situations. We assume that he always had some concrete purposes in saying what he had to say, albeit the resulting utterance usually embraced a perspective which transcended those motives. So, too, the reader may misunderstand our intention in asking which group in Rome Paul was addressing at each successive stage of his argument. Although we believe that each appeal is slanted in the direction of a specific faction in Rome, we also believe that this slant does not exclude the author's concern for all the factions in Rome.

Let us then move into the analysis of chs. 5–8, which formed what in many ways was the heart of the apostle's planned assault upon his objective. That objective: so to remove the animosities of Groups One and Two and the uncertainties of Group Three that all the churches in the Capital City would be able to join in the praise of God and in the joy and peace of the kingdom of God. This objective was perhaps analogous in the first century to the struggle today for ecumenical, liturgical and moral renewal among churches.

To which Groups did the apostle address this section? I believe the following is a probable, though not certain, answer: ch. 5 is addressed to all groups; ch. 6 primarily to Group Two; 7.1–8.17 primarily to Group One; 8.18–39 to all groups, but with special thought for Group Three. We will analyse seriatim the evidence for this answer.

Why do we interpret ch. 5 as an appeal to all the house-churches in Rome? First, we note that there is no noticeable shift in audience from the end of ch. 4, where the argument dealt with all believers. At the beginning of ch. 4, the apostle's first person (we, our, us) had linked him directly to Abraham's children according to the flesh, but by the end of the chapter his use of the first person linked him to all his readers. There is no shift in the implied content of the *we* in 5.1ff. Secondly, the typological image employed in ch. 5 is Adam rather than Abraham. I believe this change stems from the desire to deal with the universally human elements in the situation before and after faith came. The Adamic image would be more germane to the situation of Gentiles than the Abrahamic image. There are, to be sure, secondary qualifications which would be most cogent to Group One, as, for example, the mention of differences made by the coming of the Law (5.13, 20); but the fact that these are parenthetical remarks strengthens the probability that the central argument is addressed to the wider audience. Third, there are clues provided by key words which had become fighting words in Rome. We call attention to four: the weak (v.6), the sinners (v.8), boasting (v.11), condemnation and life (v.18). Let us examine some of these.

'While we were yet helpless' is the RSV translation of 5.6. *Helpless* is, however, the translation of the Greek word, ἀσθενής, which in every other instance in Romans is translated by *weak* (4.19; 8.3; 14.1f.). This word, as we have seen, was a libel used by the strong to show their scorn for their more scrupulous antagonists. I believe that in 5.6 it would have its maximum force as a reminder to Group Two concerning the universal state of all believers when Christ died for them. More especially, the gospel declares God's love for all the despised members in Group One. This hypothesis is strengthened by the apostle's parallel use of *sinners* in v.8. This term was the epithet used by Group One in condemning members of Group Two. This was their excuse for judging those Christians (14.3, 10, 13) and for trying to convert them to a decent respect for law (2.12–24). Apart from such conversion, these sinners were destined for nothing but the wrath of God (v.9). We conclude that Paul's appeal in this strategic paragraph was addressed especially to members of Groups One and

Two. It was while we were all 'sinners', while we were all 'weak', that Christ died for us. Those labels therefore lose their poison.

The same subtle logic may be illustrated by the use in this same paragraph of the word for boasting: 'We also boast in God through our Lord Jesus Christ' (v. 11). Here again the RSV obscures the original verbal links. The same Greek word (καυχάομαι) is used here as in 3.27; 4.2; 5.2f.; and 15.17. Its basic meaning is to boast in, or to take pride in, one's position or possession. Paul attacked the pride which both groups took in their special standing by asserting over and over again that it was only through Christ, only through strength furnished by God's grace, only through hope and faith (and not through their own separate status) that brothers could boast (5.2f., 11; 15.17). In 3.27 and 4.2 he had stressed this fact for members of Group One. Here in 5.1–11 he stressed it as a truth equally applicable to all believers. By dying for us when we were 'sinners' or 'weak', Christ had destroyed our reliance either on our righteousness or our strength – the respective grounds of boasting of Groups One and Two. And this boasting was more than a matter of personal status. 'It is a question of knowing what we make the basis of our life, what gives it its *raison d'etre* and value, in the sight of God for the believer, as well as in his own eyes and in other people's.'[1]

The same universality of appeal may be seen in the use of the terms for condemnation and life in 5.15–21. Group One had been accustomed to think of the libertarians of Group Two as being subject to sin, death, and condemnation. In the heat of polemics, Group Two had relied upon justifying its own freedoms by appeals to God's gift of grace, righteousness and life. To the first Paul was attempting to show that *all* Christians, including themselves, had been subject to the same condemnation and that only God's grace had acquitted them. To the second he insisted that all Christians, including the weak in faith, had been granted the same boon of eternal life and a share in the kingdom through 'the one man' (5.17). We conclude, then, that in this stage of his argument Paul addressed members of Groups One and Two concerning the status, both before and after faith, of *all Christians*, with a view to destroying their invidious pretensions to superiority.

All, not some, had been weak. All, not some, had been sinners. All, not some, had been God's enemies. In this respect, all had shared fully in the sin of Adam, in God's condemnation, in the reign of death. None of them could claim superiority over the others. Even the introduction of the Law had increased rather than lessened the guilt of men under the Law (5.20). The apostle thus sought to reject the claim to distinction on the part of any believer, a claim which he might base on his earlier situation, whether in terms of the possession of the Law or of freedom from its demands. Their union in the one man Adam had decisively established their equality.

The union in the one man Jesus Christ also decisively determined equality in their status after faith came. Here again the term *all* marks the accent of the argument, in each case implying a rejection of partisan claims that only *some* brothers had received the benefit of Christ's work (5.18f.). What had become accessible to any had become accessible to all: justification, peace, boasting, joy, grace, love, the Holy Spirit, salvation, reconciliation, acquittal, life. In the case of none of these free gifts could any of the parties in Rome claim anything special. Their unity and equality in Christ's life was as complete as their unity and equality in Adam's death. All had been dead, all were now alive.

Thus far, the argument appears to rest upon an antithetical-parallel structure in which death and life, condemnation and acquittal, were treated as equivalent opposites. Once sin had reigned in death, now righteousness reigned in life (5.17). Although this basic symmetry characterized both Paul's view of reality and his literary style, he was forced to qualify that symmetry by adding three asymmetrical elements:

1. The contrast was not simply one of past versus present status, for the present is characterized by suffering, difficulties and the need for endurance. All believers had been saved *in hope*. As much as in the case of Abraham (4.18, 20) their faith was being validated by hoping against hope (5.2, 5, 9, 17). In some ways their existence seemed more turbulent and tormented than it had been before faith came (for example, in the Christian house-churches in Rome); what was different now was their common boasting in a hope which thrived on such conflict (5.2, 5). This hope included a hope for the salvation of their alienated brothers (5.1–5 is as other-directed as 14.4, 7–9).

2. The apostle unbalanced the logical symmetry by introducing his 'how much more' refrain. Christ was not simply another Adam, equal in status and power. It was not enough to say: 'Once we

shared Adam's death, but now we share Christ's life.' Christ's death was more efficacious than Adam's, his life than Adam's. As a result, the confidence of all Christians and their hope of sharing the glory of God depended on understanding how much more powerful the grace of God had become in being channelled through Christ's death (5.9f.). In many important respects, there-fore, 'the free gift is *not* like the trespass' (5.15). This amendment was directly relevant to the disputes in Rome. Only when *all* partisans had this confidence in the power of Christ to save their *opponents* would they be able together to enjoy his joy and peace.

3. A third amendment to the symmetrical character of the Adam-Christ typology was the apostle's recognition that another factor had complicated the simple duality. This factor, appearing during the period between Abraham and Christ, was Moses' intro-duction of the Law (5.14, 20). This recognition was required both by the apostle's own experience as a Jew, and by the legitimate convictions of Group One. But this concession was not allowed to weaken his argument. The Law had made a difference in whether sin was 'counted' (5.13f.) but this did not affect the universal reign of death. The addition of the Law actually increased the extent of sin rather than diminishing it, making all the more in-escapable for members of Group One a recognition of their solidarity in Adam with their Gentile brothers and consequently their dependence upon Christ along with their Gentile brothers.

One thing, then, is certain. In this chapter Paul was describing the status of all believers, before and after conversion. Another thing is probable, that he was speaking primarily *to* partisans in Rome who by their actions rejected solidarity with one another. It was in connection with that argument that he tried to meet in advance the caveat of Group One with regard to the effect of the Law upon the condition of Jews and Gentiles before Christ came.

Having thus refuted the objections raised by Group One, the apostle turned, in ch. 6, to deal with the dangerous inferences from his arguments which had been drawn (or would be drawn) by the extremist leaders of Group Two. Let us first summarize the evi-dence for concluding that it was this group which Paul had primarily in mind.

The basic clue is provided by the slogan cited in 6.1: 'Let us continue dwelling in sin in order that grace may abound.' Here Paul is obviously quoting one of the factions. Which one? This could be a polemic thrust by members of Group One, attacking the blatant licentiousness of Group Two, an attack similar to their accusation against Paul in 3.8. Or it could be a quotation of a rationalization advanced by members of Group Two to justify their continued indifference to the Torah. This was the inference which they were in the habit of drawing from such assertions as Paul had made in 5.17–21. Such an inference was perfectly logical and was perfectly designed to madden the members of Group One. Was Paul then aiming at defending those against whom this libel was falsely attributed, as in 3.8? Or was he at this point aiming at correcting the perspectives of those who were citing this rationalization in self-defence?

The latter is the answer which best accords with the whole slant of this chapter. Not only does Paul immediately repudiate the position of those who are content to 'continue in sin' (note the 'by no means' of v. 2). He also goes on to demolish the logical grounds for this position by insisting over and over again that the death of Christ *for sin*, in which they had shared in baptism, had been a death *to sin*, so that baptism into his death-life required also on their part a death to sin. Some members had no doubt interpreted their death with Christ as conveying to them freedom from sin in a sense which the apostle deplored (6.7). He wanted to undercut that error by tracing the true freedom *from sin* to their own act of dying *to sin* (6.11). Apart from such an act, sin would retain its tyranny over them. They could become free from it only by becoming slaves of God (6.22). The necessity of dying to sin is the fulcrum of the whole chapter.[2] The argument of the chapter is not a hypothetical exercise but a serious effort to refute a position which in Paul's judgment not only endangered the freedom of Group Two, but also prevented their reconciliation with Group One, and made very precarious the situation of Group Three.

There are other clues pointing to this understanding of the dialogical partners in ch. 6. For example, when the apostle begins to speak to another faction, he makes that transition clear. Whereas ch. 6 speaks to those who claim to be 'not under the Law' (6.14f.), ch. 7 addresses those who 'know the Law' (7.1). The former group needs to 'die to sin', the latter group needs 'to die to the Law'. In arguing with the former group Paul appeals not to the Law but to their experience of baptism into Christ; in arguing with the latter the central appeal is to their experience under the Law.[3]

Such an understanding of the dialogue is supported by a possible reading of 6.15: 'Let us sin because we are not under law but
grace.' It may be that this, like the similar slogan in 6.1, is a direct
quotation from a leader of Group Two, who would say in effect:
'We have never been under the Law. Why should we put our
necks under that bondage now that we are under grace? Baptism
should not require becoming righteous by the Law's standards.'
Such an argument Paul countered with the blunt declaration that
their emancipation entailed nothing less than a new enslavement
to righteousness (6.18).

The death of Christ had been a death to sin (6.10); this was not a
repeated dying but a single final decision. In union with him, their
death also had been to sin (6.2, 4f., 7, 11, etc.); baptism had been
in fact a crucifixion of their former ego. Were they freed by faith?
Yes, but freed from sin in order to walk in newness of life, having
been made alive to God in Christ Jesus.

We should not fail to notice the connections between the central
demand of this chapter (to die *to sin* in order to live *to God*, vv. 10f.)
and the key axioms in dealing with the problems of 14; 7–9.
This English preposition *to*, as the translation of a Greek dative,
becomes quite decisive for the contour of the thought in both
passages. R. Tannehill is quite right in stressing the notion of
ownership and lordship as essential to this dative. To die *to* is to
leave the dominion in which you are the property or slave of a
particular master.

It is the powers operative in a dominion which determine its nature,
which mark it off from another dominion in which other powers are
operative. Such a dominion is a power field.[4]

This is why the giving of thanks was so decisive a factor in 14.1–9,
and why the ego-centred justifications in 6.1, 15 so alarmed Paul.

The chapter breaks into two sections – one descriptive and one
hortatory. In the descriptive section Paul used the identifying *we*
(6.1–10) to set forth the kind of freedom which all baptized believers received in dying with Christ. In the hortatory section
(6.11–23) he separated himself from the libertarian extremists
(Group Two) by using *you* and *your*. (The force of this transition
would not go unnoticed by members of Group One.) We should
not make the mistake of underestimating the numerical strength of
this faction in Rome. Paul was not setting up straw men in order

to fight them. He knew how stubbornly such convictions were held and how firmly they were defended by appeals to the emancipating cross. Yet he knew that as long as the strong in faith remained unchanged, they would continue to repel fellowship with the weak and would alienate the weak even further by open demonstrations of freedom from Law. Paul had no other alternative but to debate with them, beginning on the common ground of the gospel (ch. 5) but ending by stressing a totally different conception of its commands (ch. 6).

The transition in 7.1 is obvious. Where the author had been addressing the strong in faith, he now turns to his brothers according to the flesh who 'know the Law'. For the first group, baptism into Christ had involved death to sin; but for the second the immediate break was described as death to the Law. This contrast had been due to the fact that before faith came, the latter had lived under the Law, had been bound to it as a wife to her husband (7.2), while the former had not lived under it (6.14). Yet both had shared in the dying of Jesus, in living again with him, and in the new life of the Spirit (6.4; 7.6). For both there had been a genuine emancipation from former captivity, either to sin (6.17) or to the Law (7.6). Whereas the former dialogue in ch. 6 had tried to correct false implications which members of Group Two had drawn from the understanding of grace (5.17-21), the dialogue in ch. 7 now turns to false implications which members of Group One had drawn concerning the character of that righteousness to which all the baptized were enslaved (6.17-19). Paul now speaks directly to all believers in Rome who had been bound to the Law but who had not completely died to it.

What was his objective in addressing them? How did he hope to change them? What were they doing which he wanted them to stop? The first answer accords with our earlier analysis of ch. 14. The logical conclusion of his argument in ch. 7 is '*Therefore*, there is now no condemnation for those who are in Christ Jesus' (8.1). This was precisely Paul's objective in dealing with the weak in faith: he wanted them to stop condemning their adversaries as sinners. 'Who are you to pass judgment on the servant of another?' (14.4). Moreover, when we ask what reasons the weak gave to themselves for such condemnation, there is a certain answer: their Gentile brothers were ignoring, despising and flouting the commands of God's Law. It was loyalty to that Law that impelled the weak in faith into disrupting the community. Paul, then, wanted them to stop this condemnation. But only if their attitudes towards the Law were first changed would they stop.

That complex of attitudes had been more fully described in Rom. 2. In summary, when they condemned others, the judges had been condemning themselves (2.1). But they had been quite unaware of this self-condemnation. They had been deceived. They had practised the condemnation of others as a result of relying upon the Law. It was the Law which had prohibited theft, adultery, idolatry, blasphemy (2.21–24). It was instruction in the Law (2.17) which had induced them to adopt the role of judges. It was this self-deception which the Law had produced and encouraged which formed the target for Paul's argument in ch. 7. As long as it persisted, these brothers remained captives to 'the law of sin' and 'the body of death', and they could be emancipated only when they would recognize that they had been 'discharged from the law', when they had died to 'the old written code' which had enslaved them (7.6).

To view baptism as an act of dying to the Law was, however, an idea intolerable to the weak in faith. They heartily agreed with Paul's requirements of the Gentiles that they must die to sin (6.12f.). But they could not think of the Law as a form of slavery, comparable to the sin of the Gentile Christians. 'The Law is sin.' This is what members of Group Two seemed to be saying. It is also what Group One supposed was Paul's position. This he stoutly denied, agreeing with them as to the holiness of the Law (7.12). The problem he faced was both logical and psychological. How could he logically insist that they must die to the Law, if the Law is such a holy and good thing? What kind of argument would be effective in changing their minds towards the Law?

One step in meeting the latter need was Paul's full identification with his adversaries. Just as in dealing with Gentile Christians Paul adopted the first-person pronouns (6.1), so, too, with Jewish Christians (7.5f.). This fact has caused endless discussion among interpreters. In using the 'I' was the apostle presenting a hypothetical case or was he speaking of his own personal experience? If the latter, had he experienced this slavery before or after conversion? These questions are not relevant to our immediate concern here. In either case, the apostle was engaged here in a debate with able antagonists, and his argument, whether based on his own experience or not, was designed to persuade them to change their attitudes towards the Law and thus to correct their resulting behaviour vis-à-vis their Christian brothers.

It was the Law which had aroused sinful passions and the desires to sin according to Paul. As an example of these passions he chose covetousness (ἐπιθυμία). The command gave a person knowledge that coveting was sin, it made him aware of the danger, and thus provided sin with its opportunity. We should ask whether there was any special reason why Paul should here choose coveting as an example of sin. I believe there was. He had used the same Greek word in 1.24 to refer to the basic sin of the Gentile world – their refusal to honour God as God and to give him glory, gratitude and wisdom. He had also used it in 6.12 referring to Gentile Christians who were tempted to use the new life in the Spirit as an alibi for uninhibited behaviour. In 13.9 the prohibition of covetousness was used in immediate conjunction with the command to love the neighbour, an action which accomplished the fulfilment of the whole Law. This suggests that coveting was a form of hating the neighbour.

Paul asserted (7.11) that sin used the Law for its own purpose of deception. The command promised life; but sin used it to bring death. Of what was he speaking here? How had this deception operated? I believe the best conjecture is this: Paul was thinking of the kind of opportunity and deception which had been at work in the case of the Jewish judges as described in ch. 2. Their instruction in the Law had induced them to accuse their Gentile brothers of blasphemy as defined by the Law, and had thus caused God's name to be blasphemed among the Gentiles. They had coveted by presuming upon the kindness of God (2.4). This covetousness had led them to steal his prerogative to judge. 'The very commandment' which had promised life had thus become the occasion of their death. At this point Paul may have been thinking of his own obedience to the Law during the period when, as a judge, he had persecuted the Law-breaking Messiah by persecuting his Law-breaking disciples.

Such an accusation against the Law was bound to be offensive to members of Group One. Paul would seem to be saying 'The Law, even though good, deals out nothing but death' (7.13). Paul again replied by distinguishing between sin and the instruments of its deception. To paraphrase his argument:

Sin uses what is good. That is the mark of its sinfulness. That is what makes it so infinitely treacherous and dangerous. It takes such control of a person, that when he wants to obey the Law of God he ends by obeying the law of sin (7.25). The very wish to do right brings into play the powers of evil. When you think you are obeying the Law, you become slaves to the body of death because this obedience has been used by sin to deceive you, to kill you (7.11), and to produce the antithesis of your conscious intentions. But if you have died with Christ, if you really belong to him, you have died to this tyranny of the Law (7.4).

Again, we must ask whether Paul had in mind any specific sin on the part of his Roman readers. And again the most probable answer is: the sin of condemning their Christian brothers (8.1; 14.4) as proof of their own obedience to the Law (2.17–24). It was this sin which made so acute the dilemma of Jewish Christians, the fact that their delight in the Law of God made even more binding their slavery to the law of sin. Paul fully identified himself with them in sharing both this slavery and this emancipation. But the essential mark of this emancipation was a refusal any longer to allow the Law of God to serve as a tool by which Sin and Death could induce those in Christ Jesus to condemn their brother Christians (8.1f.). It was his desire to secure this refusal that prompted Paul to appeal in such harsh terms to his 'brothers' who knew the Law (7.1). Yet he applied the same harsh terms to himself, hoping that they would join him in his own confession. Otherwise, the same sin would trap him in his self-righteous condemnation of them. The body of sin and death, a body which was shared by unconverted Jews and Gentiles, by converted Jew and Gentiles, by apostles and believers – this body was the universal legacy for all the sons of Adam (5.12f.). If any could be delivered from this body, then that deliverance must be extended to all. Any claim to the special favour of God, any condemnation of outsiders, would illustrate that very presumption which marked the unbroken power of sin and death.[5]

Chapter 7 even concluded with this strong assertion that because of captivity to the flesh there could really be no substantial or permanent distinction between Groups One and Two (the argument is very similar to the thrust of 1.18–3.20). Chapter 8 began with the assurance of the gospel that this captivity to the flesh had been broken for all believers without distinction (similar to the emancipation celebrated in 3.21–4.25). The early paragraphs of this chapter, however, continue the dialogue with the weak in faith. We now call attention to several indications of this fact.

To those accused of condemning their 'lawless' brothers, Paul insisted: 'No condemnation.' To those ridiculed because of their weakness in faith, Paul asserted that it was not they who were weak, but that weakness and impotence came from the ways in which the flesh had distorted the Law. (It is noteworthy that in 8.3 two words are used which in 14.1 and 15.1 are the chief identifications of Group One – ἀδύνατος and ἀσθενέω.) Yet to these brothers who were so concerned to see the Law vindicated he gave the assurance that the just requirement of the Law had already been fulfilled 'in us'. Such fulfilment, which had been beyond the reach of men because of the flesh, had been accomplished by God himself and made accessible by the Spirit (8.3f.). This accomplishment had required not the condemnation of men but the condemnation of 'sin in the flesh'. The whole argument becomes very concrete and relevant when we define this particular 'sin in the flesh' as the tendency to condemn fellow-Christians as an act of supposed loyalty to God's Law. Those who 'want to please God' (8.8) can never please him by such an act.

How, then, had God condemned this particular 'sin in the flesh'? There is a double answer, both parts of which are essential for Paul's objective. (1) God had sent his own son 'in the likeness of sinful flesh'. Perhaps this can be interpreted as a way of saying 'You (Group One) would have condemned Jesus as a sinner for the same reasons you condemn other believers (Group Two)'. (2) God sent his son 'for sin' (περὶ ἁμαρτίας). This phrase *for sin* has been understood as tantamount to saying 'He sent his own son as a way of dealing with sin, as a way of atoning for sin, as a way of freeing men from sin.' In any case Paul had in mind the radical contrast between the behaviour of God vis-à-vis sin and the behaviour of men in Group One. Members of that group could be delivered from 'the mind of the flesh' (8.5) only when they had 'died to the Law through the body of Christ' (7.4). They could never become God's sons except by fulfilling the Law in the way indicated by Jesus (8.3), by joining him in the suffering entailed by redemption from the body of sin and death (8.12–17; 7.21–25). The apostle's rebuke to the self-deceived legalists was therefore as direct and sharp as he could make it. But the rebuke ended in powerful affirmations concerning the power of God to free these very brothers from 'the spirit of slavery' which impelled them 'to fall back into fear' (8.15). Moreover, his polemic against this one group was so deeply grounded in the gospel that the same argument had relevance to all groups within the church, not only in Rome but in all other places. By the time he dictated 8.17, the author seems no longer to be struggling with the ways in which sin has corrupted loyalty to the Law, but with the destiny of all the sons of God. This is why, when congregations listen to this familiar chapter, they seldom sense the importance of its original setting nor do they realize its power as a bit of polemic. In reading 8.18–39, therefore, it usually seems quite beside the point to raise question concerning the original target.

When we ask that question, the basic answer must be that Paul was addressing all Roman Christians. His *we* included all the 'heirs, of God and fellow-heirs with Christ'. Not only did he speak to all, but he spoke about all. There is a secondary answer, however which should not be neglected. I believe that in this climax of the letter Paul was speaking to the doubters and waverers, those who were in danger of 'stumbling' because of their vulnerability to pressures from right and left. Groups One and Two were confident of their respective positions and aggressive in attacking one another. As we noticed earlier, they were chiefly effective in winning converts from Group Three. But Paul was especially solicitous for the faith of this latter group, so solicitous that his anger was hot against those who were self-righteously bent on causing their 'ruin'. It is to such fearful and uncertain brothers that the closing section of ch. 8 was designed to speak with special force.

1. *8.18–25.* They could not consider 'the sufferings of the present time' with such poise as Paul could (8.18). If sin were as deeply rooted in the flesh as had been argued, on what grounds could they hope for its defeat? Must they not be able to see clear evidences of the redemption of 'our bodies'? This paragraph is so slanted as to suggest that Paul sided with them in recognizing the bondage of decay and the inward travail of Christians. They were, however, entirely unable to share his confidence in impending liberation from bondage, his ability to hope for what could not be seen, and his patient waiting for cosmic redemption. He desired to evoke in them this confidence and endurance.

2. *8.26–30.* With his *we*, Paul placed himself among those who

were tormented by their ignorance, their sense of inadequacy and inferiority, their sense of insecurity. In the midst of such wavering it was they who were therefore vulnerable to the enticements of the libertarians or the condemnation of the legalists. Conceding the legitimate basis for weakness, the apostle assures them of the intercessory power of the Spirit and of the invincible purpose of God to glorify all (not some) of those whom he had called. Moreover, this intention of God remains effective in all, not some, situations.

3. *8.31–39.* Here the apostle made explicit the thrust of his argument. Charges have been brought against some of God's elect. Some have been condemned (that 'technical term' which designated Group One) by men who presumably claimed God's authority for this condemnation. Those who are 'against us', who 'separate us from the love of Christ', implicitly contend that God gave up his son, not for all but only for those who demonstrate their obedience to the Law or their freedom from it; or they contend that he restricts his grace to those who display their worthiness. Such a mode of argument was designed to be most germane not to self-assured partisans but to diffident and uncertain waverers, whose faith was subject to attacks from both sides, whose trust was not kept between themselves and God (14.22) so that their behaviour did not proceed from faith.

All parties in Rome were deficient in hope. In ch. 4 the apostle had urged the Jewish Christians to emulate the hope of Abraham. In ch. 6 (vv. 5–11) he had wanted Gentile Christians to consider themselves dead to sin and alive to God. Now in ch. 8 he sought to impart to the fearful of Group Three a stronger confidence in the power of Christ to overcome every enemy. Nowhere did he ask Jews to live like Gentiles or Gentiles like Jews; but he demanded that all recognize that God had marked them all for the same destiny. It was in hope that they had been saved. Sharing alike in the bondage of creation to decay, sharing as well the troubles intrinsic to discipleship (v. 36), they shared above all in the victory of Christ. Paul was the first theologian of hope, in part because he traced the conflicts in Rome to Christian groups whose faith had not yet produced in them a hope as strong as that of Abraham.

There are two ways of reading this powerful chapter, ways which depend upon the implicit weight given to the phrase 'the sufferings of this present time' in 8.18. A somewhat exclusive way limits these sufferings to the more obvious persecutions of Christians by outsiders, such violence as had been used in Rome by Claudius and would soon be used by Nero. A more inclusive way includes 'all suffering which the Christian experiences . . . all the sufferings involved in creation's slavery to corruption'.[6] It is likely that the apostle chose the more inclusive way. In fact, I believe that he included in these sufferings all the travail caused by the pattern of alienation among the groups in Rome. More particularly I think he had in mind the agonized sense of confusion, weakness and anxiety on the part of Group Three, a group unable to face the future with that confidence which the apostle tried to communicate (8.26f.)

NOTES

[1] M. Bouttier, *op. cit.*, p. 16.

[2] R. Tannehill, *Dying and Rising With Christ*, Berlin, 1967, p. 9.

[3] The use of *agnoiete* in 6.3 and 7.1 indicates that in both cases an appeal is being made to what is common knowledge, to what is accepted by the group being addressed, and to what can therefore serve as a basis for further argument. Cf. R. Tannehill, *op. cit.*, p. 13. This argument will concern the incompatible inferences drawn by the different parties from this common ground, in this case baptism into Christ.

[4] R. Tannehill, *op. cit.*, p. 19.

[5] Essential to the position of his opponents was a view of sin and death which had not been affected by Christ's death. Essential to Paul's position was a view which had been drastically altered. Cf. my essay 'The Truth about Sin and Death' in *Interpretation* 7 (1953), pp. 142–55.

[6] R. Tannehill, *op. cit.*, p. 114.

V

THE ETERNAL TRIANGLE: REBUTTAL
IN 9.1–11.36

WHEN a reader attempts to organize the Epistle to the Romans according to topics and themes, he finds his task a simple one in dealing with chs. 9 through 11. There is a sharp, almost brutal break at 8.39. Leaving one topic and one manner of speaking, the author appears to have moved without warning in a totally different direction. The same roughness in transition is to be observed at 11.36. Between the two high fences enclosing these chapters, the terrain seems to be continuous and unbroken. There is a single theme: God's ways of dealing with Israel. At first sight it seems that chs. 8 and 12 have nothing to do with that subject.

However, the student who recalls that he is reading a letter which has been made complex because it was addressed to a scattered and divided audience may be inclined to ask whether the transitions are so abrupt after all. In ch. 9 did Paul shift from one dialogue partner to another? I believe the answer is no. The first shift in this regard is plainly marked in 11.13. If, then, he continued to deal with the same group in the Roman communities, but simply moved from one polemical point to another in his debate with them, what may have occasioned that movement? May his argument in ch. 9 have been shaped as a response to their anticipated rejoinder to his previous discussion? I believe that the emphatic tone and the vigorous disavowals in 9.1–6 disclose that he was indeed responding to an accusation (whether actual or only anticipated is immaterial). I think also that this accusation can be identified as coming from that group in Rome which was the primary target for 8.18–39. Let the reader consider the following matters.

Which groups in Rome would be most deeply concerned over the question of the justice or injustice of God's dealings with

Israel? Those Christians who were nearest to Israel in emotional attachments and theological perspectives – i.e. Groups One and Three. These two groups are those most immediately in view in ch. 8. Which groups would be most probable either to advance or to entertain that set of accusations which the apostle tried to refute? Assuming that he was responding to real and not fancied attacks, we may reconstruct the pattern of those attacks as follows:

When this apostle claims to love his Jewish kinsmen, he is a liar (9.1f.). He has completely cut himself off from his own brothers and deserves to be accursed (v.3). He has become a traitor to them, by denying openly the validity of their call, the covenants, the Law, the worship, and the promises (v.4). He has betrayed the patriarchs and ignored the fact that Jesus came as the Messiah of Israel (v. 5). He has gone over to the Gentiles because he believes that 'the word of God has failed' (v.6). He even contends that many Jews are bogus and that many uncircumcised Gentiles are authentic sons of Abraham (v.8). He has no desire to save Jews and makes no attempt to do so; but instead he continues to antagonize members of the synagogue (10.1). According to his gospel God has rejected Israel and accepted Israel's age-long enemies. If this were true, God would be terribly unjust. He would be taking no account of Israel's sacrifices through the centuries but would be treating the Pharoah as if he were as good as Moses (v. 17). Paul claims openly that God has rejected his people because of their sins (11.1), even though logically God should find no fault with them, inasmuch as he gives his mercy to whatever nation he wishes without respect to merit. The worst Gentiles have a right to salvation, whereas the most faithful Jews have lost that right. Paul thus abolishes distinctions between those who care nothing for the Law and those who care everything for it, thus making Christ a tool for destroying the Law, 'the end of the law' (10.4).

The vigour with which Paul responded to this portrait, accepting some charges but rejecting others, is evidence for its existence. Who painted it? Probably unconverted leaders of the numerous synagogues in Rome. Their hostility alone, however, would not have disturbed the apostle so deeply. It is probable that this portrait had been accepted by some Christians, leaders of Group One. It was this kind of attack which probably constituted the 'condemnation' with which Paul dealt so directly in chs. 2 and 14. Paul had not been the only leader to draw such fire in Rome.

We must go on to ask where his accusers would find the readiest market for these charges. This is an important question. The answer is that those most vulnerable to these attacks would be members of Group Three. We have seen that Paul was most deeply fearful of their fate as prizes in the tug of war between Groups One and Two (cf. above, p. 12). We have also seen that it was uncertainty and internal confusion among members of Group Three which made them susceptible to these pressures and in real danger of losing their faith. The apostle felt that he must, for their sakes in particular, refute the charges which had been made against him and against leaders of Group Two in Rome.

When we reconstruct the lines of battle in this way we find substantial links between chs. 8 and 9. Not only does the dialogue remain constant: Paul versus Group Three. The issues remain continuous as well: e.g. the questions of what the Law could or could not do, how the just requirements of the Law have been fulfilled, how men become sons of God, how Christ has placed all believers beyond the reach of condemnation, how the love of Christ has made Jews and Gentiles fellow-heirs of Israel's destiny. It was precisely these claims, set forward in ch. 8 to restore the confidence of waverers, which would incite the leaders of the weak in faith to counterattack in terms of God's unique and irrevocable promises to Israel, seeking to persuade the same waverers to reject the Pied Piper's blandishments.

This traitor-apostle has been attempting to establish your hope in Christ's power to fulfil God's promises quite apart from any fulfilment of the Law. But his argument is a hoax. If he is right, the history of Israel is one long road of broken promises on the part of God. If we accept his 'theology', we must believe that Israel's hope has been futile. He talks about being saved in hope all the while he demonstrates the failure of Abraham's hope. He speaks of Gentiles as being elect. What has happened to God's election of Israel?

No line of argument would more naturally be called forth by the apostle's position as advanced in chs. 7 and 8. None would more effectively threaten the faith of members of Group Three. Something more germane than the florid rhetoric of ch. 8 would be needed by way of counter-attack to strengthen the faith of members of Group Three, especially if the pressures from the right were to take the form of active persecution (8.35). Stronger faith could be purchased only by honest and thorough analysis of the present and future state of Israel, and especially of that segment of Israel which had rejected the gospel. What had happened to God's promises and call? Could they be cancelled at God's pleasure, or were they in fact irrevocable (11.29)?

A brief detour at this point may not be amiss. Modern Christians are so accustomed to giving Paul a heroic role that they may not take the charges against him seriously. This is foolish. In the original instance, the truth rather than the falsity of the accusations must have seemed the more obvious. Certainly Paul took the charges with the greatest seriousness, whether in order to salve his wounded ego or to safeguard his Gentile mission. In a similar example of anachronism, we today are habitually inclined to accept Paul's theology as authoritative. We rarely encounter people who openly repudiate his understanding of the gospel. In reading Romans, however, we must try to return to a time when most readers would have either denied or debated its basic contentions. Then the author had to summon up all available resources to sustain his argument in this case, an argument which aimed at undermining the influence of leaders of Group One on the waverers of Group Three.

What, then, were his objectives in this battle? Surely he could not expect his adversaries to capitulate to him, nor could he consider capitulating to them. It would be foolish for him to attempt too much. He must have allowed many trivial charges to pass without rebuttal. He selected those charges which threatened the followers' faith and his own vocation. In dealing with those charges, he often conceded specific accusations against himself and also key convictions of his opponents. He did not add to the pressures on members of Group Three to swing to either extreme by observing days or diets, but rather he applied his own norm to their case: 'Let everyone be fully convinced in his own mind' (14.5). He wanted his readers to have faith strong enough to wait with patience for the hope as he outlined it in ch. 8, to do so in spite of the apparent evidence cited in ch. 9 that God had revoked his promises to Israel.

To gain credence for the argument, he first of all sought to parry the personal charges. He asserted again and again his love for his kinsmen, his sorrow over their rejection of the gospel. If such a bargain could be struck, he would accept his own damnation in exchange for their salvation. In his thinking no charge seems to have cut deeper than that of betraying his people, and he made every effort to defend his loyalty to the covenants and to the

patriarchs (9.1–5). He insisted on his fervent desire that his kinsmen be saved (10.1). Denying that God had rejected his people,
he presented himself, a fully pedigreed Israelite, as proof to the
contrary (11.1). He could hardly have done less by way of defence,
because he needed the support of this faction for his projected
mission to Spanish Gentiles! This is surely one motive for his
observations concerning the role of preachers (10.14–17).

We should not underestimate the great significance that both
Paul and his kinsmen attached to family ties. The fact that Paul was
so sensitive to the charge of treason to his kin (cf. 16.7, 11, 21)
indicates that his audience also was similarly sensitive. Probably
most of the converted Jews in Rome, and especially the members
of Group Three, had close relatives among the unconverted. They
would try to preserve their family ties. The issues at stake had
become the daily source of household tension and bitterness. They
would have responded to their heart's affection for their relatives
in ways different from Paul.

Those of us who are Gentiles need to be reminded of this
personal background for each member in Group Three.

From his childhood he had venerated the Scriptures: from his childhood he had learned that the Mosaic Law which they set forth, and the
rites and ceremonies which they enjoined, were divinely instituted. The
laws about circumcision and purification, about sabbath observance
and feasts and fasts, about clean and unclean meats – around these
ordinances and customs gathered the most sacred associations of his
childhood and the most treasured traditions of his people. . . . To
repudiate them seemed a wanton rejection of the ordinances of God, a
disregard of Holy Scripture, a denial of the continuity of the divine
order![1]

How then did Paul reply to the issues? We notice how careful
he was to support every argument by citations fron scripture, an
authority which for these factions represented the supreme court
of appeal. (This had not been necessary in dealing with Group
Two in ch. 6.) A first problem was that of defining Israel. Who
belonged to Israel? That question had to be settled before anyone
could measure God's justice to Israel. The apostle rejected a purely
objectified answer, but insisted that from Abraham on there had
been two lines of descent, only one of which, that through Jacob,
represented 'the children of the promise'. God's faithfulness
should be tested only in terms of this line (9.6–13).

To this point, one rejoinder would surely have been 'That surely makes God the source of injustice, to make his love and hate depend upon so arbitrary a choice of Jacob rather than Esau.' 'No', was the apostle's reply, 'the whole object was to reveal God's mercy as the only basis of his action. He has other goals in view than men suppose.' 'If that is true,' came the reply, 'God's punishment of the sons of Esau would have been unjustified. If their defection was due to God's hatred, why blame them?' The apostle at first tried to rule out such petulance as a denial of God's 'right over the clay' (9.19–21). But he went on to argue the case on the basis of a more complex motivation. From the beginning God had intended, by showing wrath towards his own people, to open the way for sharing his glory with his non-people. His desire to include a non-people among his sons had been the key to his patience with his own people (9.22–26). The process of election, as Paul understood it, was always open-ended. God's treatment of Israel had been designed all along to open the way for the accession of Gentiles.

This accession, however, did not cancel the promise to Israel. From Isaiah on, the prophets had warned that only a remnant would be saved. That had now happened. God had preserved some children to Abraham among the elect (9.27–29.) But the division within Israel between the many who stumbled and the few who believed was not arbitrary on God's part. He had simply applied the test which had been in force since Abraham's day, the test of faith and that which proceeds from faith (ἐκ πίστεως, cf. above, p. 55), righteousness. God had not changed the basis of the covenant with Abraham but had simply enforced it (9.30–10.4). Christ is 'the end of the law' not in the destructive but in the constructive sense that faith in him has become the benchmark of that righteousness to which God had called Israel. The inclusion of Gentiles, far from being a denial of Israel's hope, has become its confirmation.

Paul recognized that it was anti-Gentilism which motivated much of the opposition. It was his stubborn insistence on the election of Gentiles (9.24, 30), eliminating any distinction for the Jews (10.12), which was the stone of stumbling. That is why he insisted that members of Group Three must recognize that 'the same Lord is Lord of all'. On that point he could not compromise. Yet he tried to make his Christian brothers see that the deeper issue was not so much the acceptance of Gentiles but the genuine-ness of faith in this Lord. Unconverted Jews had, in fulfilment of Moses' prophecy, been angry at the inclusion of Gentiles (10.19) and had thereby proved their disobedience to God. Their rejection of Paul and his mission to the Gentiles had simply embodied that faithlessness (ἀπιστία). But why should converted Jews be dis-trait over that? Members of Group Three were more faithful to Moses than were their kinsmen critics (10.5).

The argument in 10.5–13 is of central importance in Paul's objective of strengthening the faith of the beleaguered doubters. In this respect, Paul returns to the argument of 8.18–39. 'If *you* believe in your heart . . . you will be saved.' This absolute confi-dence is validated by scripture: '*No one* who believes in him will be put to shame.' Even a third time the refrain appears: '*Everyone* who calls on the name of the Lord will be saved.' This is the positive counterpart to the negative, 'Who shall separate us from the love of Christ?' (8.35). The pressure on members of Group Three had taken the form of adding certain requirements for those who wished to be saved. Paul resisted that pressure by focusing solely upon the word of faith 'which we preach' and which is 'on your lips and in your heart'. Nothing beyond belief in that word is required. The Lord does not limit his help to some only, but bestows his riches on all who call upon him. In these trenchant statements, the apostle defended his gospel, defended the inclu-sion of the Gentiles, and defended the standing of the waverers against those attacks from the right to which they would have been most vulnerable.

Having done that, he directed a final thrust against the adver-saries. He made it clear that disobedient Israel had suffered from a God-given 'stupor', a stupor which according to scripture had represented the fulfilment of David's wish (11.7–10). At this point we should note what form their stupor had taken. Their blindness in accordance with David's wish, had been connected to their table, their food (v. 10 is a citation from Ps. 69.22). Why, one must ask, should Paul have selected this example from the many avail-able cases of Israel's blindness? Surely because members of Group One in Rome were inclined to set the barriers of table-fellowship in such a way as to exclude Gentile Christians. These members were under constant pressure from the synagogue to enforce the Torah provisions on foods and they themselves exerted constan pressure on members of Group Three to do so. The issues of ch. 14 are clearly visible here in Paul's choice of citations from scripture. In fact, Paul shows this connection by quoting from the same Psalm in 15.3.

Even so, Paul did not stop with this plain-spoken, scripture-supported warning. He was not content with any negative and final verdict upon Israel, however blind and stiff-necked Israelites might prove to be. On the one hand, God had again, as in the days of Elijah, included a much larger remnant than impatient spokesmen had supposed. On the other hand, the hardened majority of Jews who had rejected the gospel had 'by no means' stumbled so as to fall. Here the apostle rejected the whole case of his opponents. Had Israel been disobedient? Yes, and as a result the Gentiles had been enriched. But the story is far from finished. The enrichment of the Gentiles and the resulting anger among the Jews anticipate the coming of a time for 'their full inclusion'. Members of Group Three who accepted this line of argument (better, this hope) would thereby become immune to the pressures from the right. If that happened, the apostle's objective of strengthening their faith would be realized. His whole case, however, rested upon an unusual reading of the story of God's dealings with his people. In this reading God's bilateral dealings with Israel had been replaced by trilateral dealings with Israel and the Gentiles, with God's purposes operating in both directions. God's objective of including the Gentiles had been realized through the faith of the remnant and the unfaith of the majority of Israel (anti-Gentilism is thus for ever eliminated from Israel's covenant-relationship). God's objective of securing the full inclusion of Israel would be realized through the faith of the Gentiles and even through the jealous anger on the part of Israel (anti-Semitism is thus forever ejected from the gospel).

However, this latter point was not germane to the immediate audience in 9.1–11.12. It became germane to the Romans who were addressed in 11.13, 'Now I am speaking to you Gentiles.' This shift in address was very strategic; it continues, I believe, into ch. 14. Paul's new target was to counter anti-Semitism among members of Group Two in the Roman churches, those who despised and ridiculed the weak in faith. Such anti-Semitism fed anti-Gentilism. Although they may have claimed Paul's support they did not show an understanding of Paul by indulging this scorn for their scrupulous brothers. To be sure, Paul's apostolate was directed to the Gentiles and he magnified this vocation (11.13). But they must understand that, even so, his ultimate motive was to save some of his fellow-Jews by making them 'jealous' of the Gentiles. If Gentiles accepted him, they must share his love for Israel, for he took seriously 'the eternal triangle' of forces as defining his vocation. Gentile believers were obligated by their own faith, so strong in their own eyes, to consider as holy both the first-fruits (Jewish believers) and the whole lump as well (Israel as a whole, both believers and unbelievers). The measure of a strong Gentile faith would be whether the believer hoped for the salvation of all branches of this tree whose root was holy (11.13–16). Gentile reconciliation had been accomplished through the rejection of Israel, as the very existence of the Roman believers proved. God would continue to exhibit his power to raise the dead (cf. 4.17; 6.5; 8.34; 14.7–9) by his future 'acceptance' of a now-rebellious people (the word for acceptance here is the same as that which in 15.7 enjoined the action of all the Christian groups in Rome). Gentiles must therefore join the apostle in his confidence for the salvation of all Israel. Their hope and love for Israel would thus become the decisive test of the strength of their own faith.

In gratitude they must confess that it is the root (God's promise to Abraham) which supports them. Rather than gloating over the exclusion of hostile Jews, they must learn the lesson: 'You stand fast only through faith.' Boasting would be as fatal for them as for their Jewish–Christian adversaries (cf. 11.18–21 with 3.27–31). Their strength was not to be gauged by contrast with the weakness of others, but by their trust in God's power to graft back again the very branches he had cut from the olive tree. To keep them humble Paul explained to them the mystery of the eternal triangle. One side's disobedience had been the means of the other side's redemption; the other side's redemption would become the means of the first side's return. Thus there would be none who had not been disobedient, none who had not been recipients of mercy.[2] By means of this logic, the apostle reached the position of asserting that Israel, disobedient, hard-necked Israel, the enemy of God, had throughout remained beloved by God. God still loved them; so, too, should the Gentile Christians who had suffered most from their hostility. Approaching the problem by this route, Paul was ready to accept the central claim of his bitterest enemies (i.e. 'the gifts and the call of God are irrevocable') without repudiating the gospel of grace by endorsing either anti-Gentilism or anti-Semitism. For him, the measure of faith became the degree to which one genuinely hopes for the salvation of his enemy. The modern reader, reminded of the intransigence of hostile communities today, can only wonder how many in the Roman churches were found to be willing to adopt the apostle's argument.

We may be sure that many leaders of Group Two would object to the logical inconsistency in Paul's position paper, just as Gentile scholars today turn their spotlight on that inconsistency especially at two points. One focus is the future fate of Israel.

The logic of his conception of the Church demanded that Paul should not think of Israel after the flesh as having any special office, but this is somehow what he could not conceive. . . . Despite his noble universalism he finds it impossible not to assign a special place to his own people.[3]

The second point where logical inconsistency is apparent is in Paul's answers to the questions 'What advantage has the Jew? What is the value of circumcision?' According to Professor Dodd, in a passage cited with approval by W. D. Davies, 'The logical answer on the basis of Paul's argument is "None whatever."' Yet, in spite of this illogicality, Paul takes care to assert great advantage.[4]

What are we to believe? Was Paul's position permeated with hopeless inconsistencies, stemming from his emotional attachments to Israel? Or was his position based on logical inferences from the gospel which both then and now defy partisan logic, whether by Jew or Gentile? I believe the latter to be nearer the truth. But the fact that Paul has not been able to convince even the best modern scholarship of that truth should make us aware that he faced even greater difficulties in convincing the deeply involved partisans in Rome.

NOTES

[1] G. O. Griffith, *op. cit.*, pp. 9f.

[2] See 'All', a sermon preached by Karl Barth in Basel Prison; English translations in *Interpretation* 14 (1960), pp. 164–9, and in K. Barth, *Deliverance to the Captives*, London, 1961, pp. 85–92.

[3] W. D. Davies, *op. cit.*, p. 75; cf. also C. H. Dodd, *op. cit.*, p. 183.

[4] W. D. Davies, *op. cit.*, p. 76; C. H. Dodd, *op. cit.*, p. 43.

VI

THE MERCIES OF GOD: MEASURING
FAITH IN 12.1–13.14

THE exploration of our hypothesis concerning Paul's purpose in Romans is virtually complete. In each section of the letter we have asked two basic questions. To which faction among the house-churches in Rome did he address this section? How did his debate with that faction shape the course of his argument? We have seen that in the first four sections Paul addressed Groups One, Two and Three. It is obvious that there was no need for him to single out Groups Four and Five. In those groups would be found most of the leaders, saluted in ch. 16, who agreed with Paul's basic position. He viewed them as part of the solution rather than part of the problem. The case is quite otherwise with the other three factions. Each of them formed a central part of the problem. Each had the power to defeat the objectives of Paul, whether those immediately at hand in writing the letter or those anticipated after his arrival in Rome.

One thing distinguishes this next section, chs. 12 and 13, of the letter: the difficulty in finding answers to these two questions. Here there are very few echoes of the immediate quarrels in the Roman churches and almost no evidence of an address to a particular faction. Moreover, it is quite clear why this is so. These chapters seem to be a grab-bag of disconnected, unsorted teachings which do not reflect any effort at continuous argument against a sharply defined interlocutor. The teachings are so generalized that they appear to apply with equal force to all Christian readers anywhere and at any time. They represent regular catechetical instruction, not *ad hoc* pastoral counsel or apologetic polemic. They cover many separate topics. The instructions are so condensed, so proverbial in their brevity, that it is easy to conclude that their form reflects the processes of communal oral tradition rather than the immediate purposes of an individual editor.[1] All of these teachings have numerous parallels elsewhere in scripture, a fact that throws doubt upon the Pauline authorship of any of them.

Notwithstanding the cogency of these observations, I believe a case can be made for assigning these two chapters to a dialogue between the apostle and a particular faction in Rome. It would probably be safer to conclude that he was addressing all Christians without distinction. In support one could appeal to the generalized nature of the teachings themselves, to the undifferentiated character of the *you* of address ('I appeal to you, brethren'), and to the explicit: 'I bid every one among you' (12.3). Although this would be the more usual decision, I believe a bolder answer is justified by the evidence, admittedly sparse here. These chapters, in my opinion, are a continuation of Paul's dialogue with Group Two in 11.13ff., and a preparation for his appeal to the same Group in 14.1f. The presumption in reading a letter which has been addressed to various recipients should be that the author does not shift his address from one to another without giving some sign of it. Here there is no such sign. Rather, there is evidence of continuity in concern, a continuity which bridged the obvious contrasts in the form and content of the material used. Let me stress two links in the conversation.

Paul had just been appealing to the strong in faith to recognize how the mercy of God has been operating in their behalf. 'You were once disobedient to God but now have received mercy because of their disobedience' (11.30). Gentiles are therefore indebted for their salvation to the very Jews whom they now ridiculed. Moreover, God's design had an important next step: 'They have now been disobedient in order that by the *mercy* shown to you they also may receive *mercy*' (11.31). The corollary is this: Gentile Christians must accept God's appointment to this role of channelling his mercy to Israel, an acceptance which would transform their attitudes towards Jewish believers. Note that this idea was at the very forefront of Paul's mind when he went on to say, 'Therefore, by the *mercies* of God, I appeal to you, brethren. . . .' Different images came into play here; a different form of tradition was utilized. But in this context the generalized call to a renewal of the mind had a quite specialized application. The self-assured Gentile Christians in Rome, accustomed to scoff at their

Jewish colleagues, were reminded forcefully that for their worship to be appropriate (λογικήν) and for their action to be perfect (τέλειον – the vocabulary here is fitting for an address to Gentiles), they must reject that conformism to this age which had been embodied in their earlier anti-Semitism.[2]

Notice the second appeal in 12.3, an appeal with which Paul introduced the catechetical teaching regarding the body. This appeal is directly linked, it seems to me, to the conversation in 11.13f. Paul's central objective there had been to destroy the boasting of Group Two over Jews who had rejected the gospel, a boasting which enlarged their sense of self-importance, complacency, and conceit in their own wisdom (11.18, 20, 25). Paul still had that concern in mind when he dictated to Tertius, the scribe: 'I bid every one among you not to think of himself more highly than he ought to think' (12.3). To be sure, this is a generalized exhortation. It calls all believers to cut their ego down to size, but in this letter and for this group, it had a particularized thrust.

Of 12.3, Professor Schelkle correctly observes:

Since this is the first in the series of exhortations and since Paul declares it with emphatic reference to his apostolic commission, and since he directs the admonition to every individual in the community, it must have been especially urgent and *directed toward a particular phenomenon in the community* (italics mine).[3]

To these three 'sinces' I would add others: since on at least three other occasions in these two chapters humility is enjoined (12.1, 10, 16), and since elsewhere Paul 'excludes' boasting on the part of Groups One and Two (3.27f.; 11.17f.), and since those groups were alienated by the fact that each claimed superiority over the other (14.10), we can be quite certain of the nature of that 'particular phenomenon' against which Paul was directing his exhortation. He believed that the impasse would be removed if *each* group considered the *other* group superior.

For this reason, the command is buttressed by an added clause which would have had special pertinence for those who delighted in contrasting their strong faith to the weak faith of their neighbours: 'each according to the measure of faith which God has assigned him.' In other words: 'The stronger your faith, the more sober should be your self-judgment.' 'The stronger your faith, the more transformed should you be by the mercies of God' (12.1).

'The stronger your faith, the greater should be your appreciation of the grace given to others'; 'The stronger your faith, the greater should be the proportion of your service to the other members' (12.4–8). Paul's objective was to secure the help of members of Group Two in uniting the scattered cells in Rome. It was to accomplish this very special end that he utilized these standardized teachings.

We may observe the same continuity of purpose in the transition between chs. 13 and 14. It is clear that the first request in ch. 14 is addressed to the strong in faith with regard to hospitality for the weak in faith. One alternative to hospitality is 'disputes over opinions'. Paul wanted to exclude that kind of behaviour. It was precisely that kind of 'quarrelling and jealousy' which he pointedly identified among 'the works of darkness' (13.12). The other 'works', as well, were kinds of Gentile behaviour which both polluted the life of Gentile believers in Rome and vexed their Jewish brothers: 'revelling and drunkenness . . . debauchery and licentiousness' (13.13). To be sure, there remain chasms between the materials of chs. 13 and 14, especially when we think in terms of ethical themes, but there was continuity in terms of the author's dialogue with his readers, as he tried to secure modification in those types of behaviour which destroyed 'righteousness, peace and joy in the Holy Spirit' (14.17). At the beginning he described this modification in terms of conformity to the old age versus a renewal of mind appropriate to the new (12.1f.). At the end of the section he described it in terms of being clothed in the works of darkness or the armour of light. The images changed but the issues remained constant.

In interpretations of the appeal of Paul in 13.13f., modern liberal Christians are given to making two errors. They do not really accept the pictures of New Testament congregations as communities where such 'vices' were openly practised. Even less often do they visualize leaders in those communities defending and even commending such behaviour as expressions of gospel-given freedoms. Yet the tone of the apostle's appeal reminds us that such assumptions are in fact errors. Moreover, Paul's reference to the 'hour' in 13.11 intimates that probably the excitements over living in the 'last hour' had given a ready excuse for revelling to that considerable minority whom we have called Group Two. We probably should feel more empathy with them than we usually do if we are to grasp the seriousness and cogency of Paul's teaching. Moreover, we should not overlook in Paul's appraisal the relative importance of the sin of quarrelling. In the list of six 'vices' it is by no means an afterthought or foot-note, but belongs on a par with the others.

We should not forget, then, that already in chs. 12 and 13 the apostle was concerned with the disputes dealt with in chs. 14 and 15, and that he was addressing the members of Group Two who viewed their own liberties as proof of the strength of their faith, as contrasted with the weakness of their despised adversaries. The issue between them revolved around the question of how strength should be measured. On that issue, the apostle presented several tests: How fully have you presented your bodies as living sacrifices? Is your self-praise consonant with God's gift? Do you measure your achievements in terms of grace? How strong is your faith as measured by love of those who condemn you; by returning their curses with blessings? How clearly is your behaviour consistent with the dawning of a new day? Are you strong enough to overcome the compulsive habits of coveting and jealousy?

When a reader keeps this situation in mind he will notice a new pertinence in many of the generalized injunctions in the intervening paragraphs. 'Let love be genuine . . . love one another with the affection *due to brothers* . . . try to excel each other in showing honour (not in despising the weak in faith) . . . rejoicing in the hope (the *one* hope according to which God will have mercy on *all*, 11.32) . . . enduring patiently persecution (from Jews and even Jewish brothers) . . . persevering in prayer (for your 'enemies' the Jews 11.28) . . . having fellowship with the saints in their needs (giving financial support to Jewish believers) . . . strenuously seeking to give hospitality to strangers (opening your house-church to meetings with Jewish house-churches) . . . bless those who persecute you, who condemn you (14.4), who call you accursed (9.1), who deny you a place of equality among those who belong to Christ.'

What am I suggesting in the above emendations of the text? I do not wish to deny that these exhortations were shaped to apply to all Christians at all times. Nor am I denying that Paul, in writing this section, intended it to be read by all members of all the churches there. I am simply illustrating what special nuances and force these teachings must have conveyed to the members of

Group Two and I am suggesting further that Paul intended this.

Consider, for example, the injunction, 'Contribute to the needs of the saints.' Remember the occasion of this letter. Recall the dangers and difficulties inherent in gathering the collection for the Judean Christians from Gentile churches. Notice that Paul used here precisely the same terminology in referring to that contribution (15.25f., 31). Ponder the fact that this collection has been specified as a major factor in the approval of the Gentile mission by the pillar apostles in Jerusalem (Gal. 2). Against that background, Paul's appeal to the Gentile constituency in Rome to join in this kind of sharing is very significant. It bore directly upon several of his objectives. Did he ask them to send money to Jerusalem to be added to the collection from other Gentile churches? It is possible, though perhaps unlikely. Did he ask them to give aid to the Jewish house-churches in Rome, as a sort of parallel to Paul's efforts in Jerusalem? This is much more likely. Beginning with 12.14, he was clearly thinking of action towards men from whom the readers were estranged. It is altogether logical that concern with that same estrangement should have occasioned the commands in 12.9–13. Certainly the demand for hospitality fits precisely into the context we have described, a context in which the desired unity of the Roman churches absolutely required obedience to this command.

Commentators are fond of pointing out that the same Greek verb which is translated *practise* in 'practise hospitality' is translated *persecute* in 'bless those who persecute you'. If Paul intended this, it is an important pun. Is it a coincidence that it appears here in two adjacent commands? Hardly. Is its appearance to be attributed to the laws of oral tradition, according to which two separate teachings gravitate together because the same word (*Stichwort*) happens to appear in both? This may explain in part the conjunction of the two teachings here. But I believe that Paul also intended the conjunction to show that just as the word of blessing was the opposite of the curse, so, too, the pursuit of hospitality was the exact opposite of the kind of persecution which members of Group Two were suffering in Rome.

If there is merit in this suggestion we may venture to suggest also that throughout the paragraph 12.14–21 the apostle was seeking to correct the behaviour of Group Two towards fellow-Christians, in the midst of the kind of debate illustrated by 9.1–11.12

and the kind of tensions described in 14.1–15.6. The whole paragraph may be read in such a way that 15.1 becomes its logical conclusion. In this case the evil of which the apostle spoke was evil done to this faction by the other factions. The evil was such that the best rejoinder was hospitality, one congregation giving food and drink to a hostile congregation. Such action corresponded to the command of v.13, to the project on which Paul was engaged when he was dictating this letter, to the situation which constituted the acute problem in Rome (the eating and drinking together of the Christian groups), and to the eucharistic action by which the unity of the brethren might be secured.[4]

Here again the command of Paul to 'live in harmony with one another' required above all obedience to the command 'never be conceited' (12.16). It was conceit that had led them to repay evil with evil, conceit which had induced them to refuse to welcome the weak in faith, conceit which had threatened their own future as branches grafted into the olive tree (11.20f.). In this context, every command becomes applicable to the kind of behaviour-change which Paul wanted to produce among the strong in faith. Did their opponents accuse them of breaking every command in the Decalogue? Let them not worry about such accusations. Not being under the Law, they were not obliged to observe the Decalogue, including the command to observe the Sabbath (14.5). Their only debt in this regard was the love of the neighbour. If they loved those very neighbours who were accusing them of being accursed by the Law, they would actually be fulfilling that Law (13.8–10).

I would interpret in this fashion all the teachings in these two chapters excepting one – the pericope concerning obedience to the governing authorities. Here I must admit that I am unable to find particular reasons in the Roman situation for Paul's inclusion of this teaching. There are, however, several relevant observations to be noted. Gentiles were more likely to reject civil authorities than were Jews, whose tradition was very similar to that of Pauline teaching. The disrespect shown by Gentile Christians for civil authorities may have been rationalized as an expression of their new emancipation by the gospel, along with the licentiousness described in 13.13. Jewish–Christian circles may have feared guilt-by-association with such Gentile brothers, since Jews were so much more vulnerable to repressive measures by the authorities.

In one of the more recent studies of this passage, C. D. Morrison indicates his belief in the presence among Roman Christians 'of a particular pride in independence'. This group was 'not only independent of apostolic authority in particular, but was proud of its freedom from authority in general'. Vis-à-vis political institutions, it took a position 'outside or revolting from the Jewish tradition in this as well as other respects'.[5] This description fits our profile of Group Two. The policy of subjection to political authority ran counter to their proud freedom and provoked a resistance to the establishment not unlike that of Christian hippies today.[6]

These are probable factors in the situation. We do not know what were the exact circumstances which had led Claudius, a few years earlier, to expel some Jewish Christians (including Prisca and Aquila), nor do we know the circumstances which would induce Nero, a few years later, to use Christians as scapegoats whom he could with impunity accuse of setting fire to the city. We do not know what attitudes the various house-churches had taken towards the authorities. If some were composed mainly of slaves in large households, as is probable, it is quite possible that their members had become infected with the unrest which was endemic among Roman slaves during this period. Yet we don't know and we never can know enough about the situation to interpret in precise terms the occasion that led Paul to include 13.1–7. In the possibilities mentioned above there are, however, enough clues to lead the critic to suppose that in Paul's judgment members of Group Two needed this teaching and that, if they heeded it, they would contribute to the realization of those objectives which we have detailed above. We believe, therefore, that even in these chapters, where evidence is admittedly elusive and ambiguous, the conclusion is tenable: Paul was addressing the strong in faith with a view to accomplishing the objectives which he stated most explicitly in the final chapters of his letter.

Even these general teachings in chs. 12 and 13, therefore, became highly pertinent to the apostle's very specific objectives in addressing himself to Roman Christians. We do not have any evidence concerning his success in realizing those objectives. He may have failed entirely to cool the heated antagonisms among the brothers. His letter may even have put the bellows to the fire. We do not know. We know only that someone was sufficiently impressed by his argument to preserve the letter. Such preservation indicates at least a small degree of effectiveness in accomplishing the intended strengthening of faith. The best test of the letter's power, in my opinion, is whether it is capable of producing the obedience of faith among alienated groups in modern churches. The honest man will admit that there is real doubt of that capability, that is, if he considers all the evidence provided by unreconciled hostilities within the Christian community at present. Yet honesty also demands full recognition of the amazing power of Paul's faith to remain modern. So I conclude this analysis of the epistle with vigorous support for the judgment of F. C. Porter, my revered predecessor at Yale:

> It is necessary to understand the differences between Paul and Christ, and also the differences between Paul and ourselves; but the greatness of Paul consists in his likeness to Christ, and also in his likeness to us, his power and right to bridge the centuries and become our contemporary.[7]

NOTES

[1] The deficiencies in this widely-accepted approach are effectively set forth in V. Furnish, *op. cit.*, pp. 98f.

[2] V. Furnish has called attention (*Op. cit.*, p. 105) to several neglected links between 12.1f. and ch. 6. I believe that the reason for these connections may be traced to the fact that in both passages the apostle had in mind the same faction.

[3] K. H. Schelkle, *op. cit.*, p. 198.

[4] It is curious that so often in generalized teaching the apostle draws his specific examples from the area of table hospitality. Yet this is not so strange if one visualizes a situation as in 14.2f. in which dietary scruples have prevented Christian fellowship at the Lord's table, and if we recall how significant the eucharist was to the apostle as a sacrament of unity in the body of Christ (I Cor 10.16–22; 11.17–34). In ch. 11 Paul had pointed out, especially to members of Group One, how Israel had turned the holy table into a snare and a pitfall. Now he stresses especially to members of Group Two how revelling and contentiousness at their table can turn the day into night (13.13) and how, by contrast, they can by the proper use of food and drink (12.20) achieve reconciliation with their adversaries. The same table could become the table of the Lord or the table of demons.

[5] C. D. Morrison, *The Powers That Be*, London, 1960, pp. 104f.

[6] O. Michel, *op. cit.*, pp. 281f.

[7] F. C. Porter, *op. cit.*, p. xiii.

PAUL'S MISSIONARY DYNAMIC[1]

First we need to ask a seemingly gratuitous question: *Was* Paul a missionary? If so, in what sense? We ask this question because the term missionary conjures up in our mind a strange conglomeration of associations. It projects upon the screen of memory either a long line of heroes or a motley group of discredited fanatics. On such a screen Paul's image is inevitably warped. For he was not a Protestant missionary, in many of the connotations of that word. For example, when we think of missions we frequently contrast foreign and home missions. We distinguish church work that is supported by benevolent funds from parishes that are self-supporting. We recall those recurrent campaigns for funds, that item in the annual budget, or that special sermon tucked away in our files. Or we think of the mission board which selects, trains, and sends men to a particular area for a specific task. But none of these aspects of the life of a modern missionary is to be found in Paul's career. It is only by anachronistic thinking that Paul is clothed in such modern attire.

If we are inclined to force into a modern stereotype the external character of Paul's work, we are even more apt to modernize his motives, his objectives, his methods. And in this area there are few safeguards against anachronism (as Professor Cadbury has ably demonstrated in the case of Jesus[2]). Especially do we misread the sources of Paul's dynamic where those sources involve presuppositions which are either unintelligible or unacceptable to us. There is an irreducible strangeness about Paul which becomes all the clearer after we have freed him from our harmonistic thinking. Motives which seemed to him most decisive often appear to us most antiquated. And it is precisely this motivation which we are inclined to modify in order to save him for our gallery of saints. The motives wherein Paul is most completely different from us are also the motives wherein he was farthest removed from the Pharisees of his day. And our efforts to shape him to our liking usually end by making him more like the Pharisee than like the apostle.

For we should never forget that Judaism was a missionary religion, that Pharisaism was the spearhead of that mission, and that Paul was foremost among the Pharisees. And as a Pharisee his motivation is both intelligible and respectable, for it is found in many religions. In fact, it is widespread among Christians today. As it is difficult for a man to be a good man without becoming a Pharisee, it is even more difficult for a good man to be a missionary without becoming a Pharisee, and I use the term Pharisee not as a symbol of what was bad in Judaism but of what was good. Yet it was precisely his career as a Pharisee which Paul completely repudiated when Christ called him to a new mission.

Before that call, the springs of Paul's energy had been deep and powerful, attaining a maximum force on his road *to* Damascus. But on that road, God revealed to him Jesus as Messiah. And on the road *from* Damascus he was a new man. That rebirth did not mark simply the substitution of one body of propaganda for another, allowing him to preserve the same motive and method. He did not merely shift from one camp of religious imperialists to another. Ever and again he testified to a complete reversal in his vocation – in message, dynamic, objective, and method. The study of his dynamic must therefore begin with the impact of this event. What was this revolution and how did it produce a new dynamic?

The revolution was not simply a revolution in his own private experience; it was far more ultimate and objective than this. Jesus had been declared the Messiah; his death and exaltation had signalled the strategic opening of the final conflict which, now in progress, would soon be consummated in the Messiah's return to establish the kingdom. From Paul's standpoint, the death, exaltation, and return are three inseparable moments in the same event. And this event marks the boundary between two wholly different ages, the boundary between history and the fulfilment which lies beyond history. In this event all creation is reborn according to its original purpose. Here all life – whether cosmic, historical, social, or personal – moves into the realm of final judgment and redemption. Here is the gate through which God 'delivers us out of the power of darkness and translates us into the kingdom of the Son of his love'. At long last God has begun the task of reconciling the whole rebellious world to himself, and the invasion of Paul's life is but one beach-head in the invasion of all enemy territory.

But the most astounding thing was not the fact that the kingdom had now drawn near. The most astounding thing was the nature of the events through which the approach of the kingdom became manifest. For, in Jesus, the Messiah had been disclosed not as a transcendent divine being, immune to sin and death, but as an all-too-human, all-too-sinful, all-too-impotent Galilean, a scandal which reached its acme in the death on the cross. This was the incredible offence which as a Pharisee Paul had righteously resisted; it was the incredible gospel which as an apostle he was impelled to accept and preach! The most horrible event had become through God's own choice the hinge between the ages, the difference between night and day. In the cross of the Messiah, history comes to its end. This does not mean that the kingdom had been fully established but that in the sufferings of the Messiah the powers of the end-time had begun to work. Confronted by this stupendous revelation, Paul was changed from a Pharisee missionary to an apostle of Christ. His dynamic stemmed from this 'unheard-of' event, in which he was called to participate. The major changes in motivation may be summarized under three captions:

1. *The End and the Means*

When the Messiah was identified as the crucified Jesus, Paul was forced to alter his convictions concerning the means by which God brings his kingdom into history. As a Pharisee he had eagerly longed for the fulfilment of the promise and had assumed that such fulfilment awaited the full obedience to the Law. At least one of his fellow-rabbis had taught that God would usher in the new day if all Israel would observe the whole Law for as long as a single Sabbath day. It is not difficult to explain missionary zeal with such a view as this, as long as one believes that his human effort may hasten the redemption of the world. In making proselytes, Paul had probably belonged among those rabbis who taught: 'Know that the world to come is made only for the righteous.'[3] He believed that 'a proselyte who takes upon himself all the commands of the Law with a single exception is not to be admitted.'[4]

So he had given himself unstintingly to preparing Israel and himself for that Great Day.

But the spectacle of the Messiah on the cross reversed all that. The Law had been intended to lead men to Christ by making known to them their sin, not by making them secure in their righteousness. A limited means to a limited end, it could no longer be the sole means to an ultimate end. And human efforts to rely upon it for salvation had been pathetic and misguided attempts to usurp God's role as judge and to control the time and range of his salvation. Now Paul was confronted by a kingdom that came in the work of a Messiah crucified by the righteous. And his death had been the first and necessary step in the kingdom's coming. The advent does not depend upon human righteousness; nor does it await the purification of Israel; nor does it come to the good by extending the area of goodness. It is a gift of forgiveness to sinners at the point of their greatest sin. The apostle can no longer demand 'Fulfil the Law in order that the kingdom may come and that you may enter it'. He can only proclaim 'The kingdom has come, it is coming, it will come – here. Here in Christ has the divine mystery disclosed itself as power to salvation. Here alone are sin and death transcended by righteousness and life. Here alone does frustration become fulfilment.'

As a sinner whom Christ had reclaimed for his kingdom, Paul received forgiveness, justification, peace, joy – the gifts of the Spirit, the first-fruits of an age which would rapidly develop into a full harvest. Only the Spirit had made possible the initial response of faith. It speaks haltingly through the simplest words of prayer. It brings peace to the harassed soul. It defines the task of every believer and gives him needed strength for performance. It calls Paul to joyful witness and drives him out with the apostolic news. Before Damascus he had been constrained by hope of justification in the *future* kingdom; now he is constrained by the love of a *present* and *living* Messiah through whom he had received justification. Now *the end precedes the means, provides the means*. The end-time 'hastens and tarries', but its powers are now at work and will not be denied. And those who live in the new day apprehend it as a *power* that enables them to do all things, as a *love* from which nothing can separate them. This new impact of the *end* on the *means* – and the choice of the most despicable means – was the first reverberation of the revolution in Paul's life.

2. *Finality and Relativity*

A second reverberation was the realization that the kingdom in its coming shatters all claim to human advantages. In its finality it transcends all the relativities of history.

As a Pharisee Paul had cherished his advantages.

If any other man thinks he has reason for confidence in the flesh, I have more: circumcised on the eighth day, of the people of Israel, of the tribe of Benjamin, a Hebrew born of Hebrews, as to the Law a Pharisee, as to zeal a persecutor of the church, as to righteousness under the Law blameless (Phil. 3.4–6).

We may not doubt that he was grateful to God for these advantages or that he was sincere, altruistic, and self-sacrificing in his loyal efforts to extend the sovereignty of God by extending these blessings to other men.

But when God revealed his kingdom in the cross apart from such advantages, he revealed that Paul's zeal for God had been in fact a fighting against God. He had advanced far beyond his countrymen – but in the *wrong direction*. He must surrender these human advantages if he were to 'apprehend the excellency of the knowledge of Jesus'. He must henceforth count them as worthless.

Nor did he substitute a new set of human advantages as a basis for superiority. All boasting in what he possessed or in the character he had achieved was now excluded. He could only say 'I am nothing'. But this negation did not cut the nerve of exertion, for now he worked more freely and energetically than ever. 'For this I toil, striving with all the energy which he mightily inspires in me' (Col. 1.29). He had been gripped by the *power* of the Risen Lord, entangled in the fellowship of his sufferings, conformed to his death (Phil. 3.10). And it was in *this* regard that he could claim to be 'not inferior to the chief apostles'. The Spirit indeed banishes thoughts of human inferiority and superiority, for it blows where it will.

The coming of the end of history in the cross likewise made obsolete all the relative institutions and standards of history. The Pharisaic mission had been undergirded by the conviction that there existed a basic distinction between the people of God and all others. On the maintenance of this barrier rested the consummation

of history; finality would but represent the extension and comple-
tion of his wall. Paul had set himself to repair the breaches in the
wall, wherever the Law, the temple, or the covenants were
threatened. And he had been correct in recognizing the danger to
the wall from the preaching of the gospel.

It was when Paul was on the business of repairing the wall that
God manifested himself in the crucified Galilean. God declared
his intention not to establish the wall but to demolish it. When the
wall fell, Paul's vocation as a watchman on the wall 'came a-
tumblin' down' and his Jericho lay defenceless. All the walls of
human separateness and seclusion, of pride and righteousness, of
wisdom and power, were forever levelled. What a tremendous
upheaval in human history and in Paul's personal history!

Paul was made known to himself as a blind leader of the blind,
who had stumbled against the Stone and fallen into the pit. Now
he could not escape the startling fact: 'There is no distinction'
(Rom. 3.22). Small wonder that Luther should select this staccato
negation as the very centre and kernel of all scripture, or that
Barth's emphasis upon it provoked such storm. To quote from
Barth's comment on this verse:

It is precisely Paul, who, daring, in Jesus, to put his trust boldly in
grace alone, is able, in Jesus, also to perceive the divine breaking down
of all human distinctions. Indeed, Paul's courage proceeds from this
insight. Because he is Apostle of the Gentiles he is the Prophet of the
Kingdom of God. Once this interdependence was obscured, there came
into being what was afterwards known as 'missionary work.' But this
is something quite different from the mission of Paul. His mission did
not erect barriers; it tore them down. God can be known only when
men of all ranks are grouped together upon a single step; when those
of the highest rank regard 'suffering with the whole social order of
their age and bearing its heavy burden' as the noblest achievement of
which they are capable; when the rich in spirit think nothing of their
wealth – not even in order to share it – but themselves become poor and
the brothers of the poor.[5]

This abolition of distinctions was based upon another negative:
'All have sinned and fall short of the glory of God' (Rom. 3.23).
The relativities of history are not overcome by the discovery of a
finality within history. The walls that sunder race and clan are not
levelled by the discovery of a least common denominator, by a
common possession, whether of rational endowment or of benevo-

lent impulses or of religious temperament. The solidarity afforded by these human traits offers no ground for hope when one has seen their harvest in the death of Jesus and the continuing miscarriage of social existence, when one sees the best of them permeated with the idolatries of this age. Relative walls are transcended only by that kingdom which reveals man's true solidarity as being a solidarity in sin.

Genuine fellowship is grounded upon a negative; it is grounded upon what men lack. Precisely when we recognize that we are sinners do we perceive that we are brothers.[6]

It was this sense of fellowship in sin that drove Paul to proclaim the gospel. But how does 'fellowship grounded upon a negative' produce vigorous missionary dynamic? To be sure it makes Paul see the world as *One World*. But why become a missionary unless we are convinced of a truth we possess, a salvation which we can dispense, a way of life which we follow, unless we can look upon ourselves, our law, our culture, our religion as in some sense superior? Is not the problem of history to be solved only by establishing as supreme *one* moral or religious system? But all such logic was closed to Paul. For now he realized that his own life was in fact a participation in the limitations of finiteness. He could no longer hope to escape those limitations by attributing premature finality to one culture or law or religion, however perfect as measured by human standards. The problem of history could only be solved by God's act in giving the kingdom to men, regardless of relative distinctions. Indeed, God *had* solved the problem of history by sharing his own final power and love in Jesus. He had imprisoned all men in disobedience in order that he might free all. (Rom. 11.32) Thus the breaking down of all distinctions among men was the manner in which God opened the kingdom to all men.

No longer could Paul look upon men benevolently as objects of condescending compassion; no longer could he place himself on a step above them, or exalt one plane of human righteousness over all other planes. But now he could receive God's gift of forgiveness and reconciliation, life within the powerful orbit of that ultimate kingdom. Once he had been a watchman on a relative wall between two cultures and had attributed to that wall a false eternity. And in so doing he had become a prisoner of a relative culture. Now he recognizes that with all men he is a prisoner of the barriers within history. But he is a 'prisoner turned watch-man' (Barth), for he stands on the boundary not between two human institutions, but between two ages. Between the kingdom of God and all the kingdoms of this age there is an 'absolute qualitative distinction' which blots out all other distinctions. On that mountain range stands the cross, and those who wish to stand there must share the sufferings of the Messiah. They must die to themselves and their world; then it is that God raises them from that death and enables them to stand with Jesus as a sign of the kingdom's ingress. To them God gives the vocation of watchmen on this new and ultimate boundary.

3. *Watchmen of the End*

Let us examine more closely the vocation of this watchman. Clearly he must confront men with the news that they stand in 'the time between the times', in the crisis of decision and judg-ment. He must call them to flee from the coming wrath and assure them of God's offer of forgiveness. He must so tell the story of the passion that it is apprehended as universal judgment upon men's sin and men's righteousness, that it may prompt them to a radical repentance of both their sin and their righteousness.[7] To be as radical as the cross, repentance must mean a complete dying to the world and the standards of the world. He must so tell the story of the exaltation that it is apprehended as the final triumph of God over the world, a triumph which through God's grace can be appropriated by sinners who have faith. He must point to the signs of the kingdom's power in the gifts of the Spirit, living evidences of the activities of the Risen Lord. He must receive and communi-cate the words which the Spirit supplies. The recipient of love, he must embody it – fulfilling the law of Christ by bearing the burdens of others. To himself, and to those who believe through his word, he must insist that the whole pattern of life to its smallest detail be appropriate to the new ground of existence. 'If we live by the Spirit, let us also walk by the Spirit' (Gal. 5.25). Himself reconciled to God in Christ, he must carry out whatever ministry of recon-ciliation the Spirit directs, 'Necessity is laid upon me; woe to me if I do not preach the gospel!' (I Cor. 9.16). This necessity was laid upon Paul. He became a missionary to the Gentiles; he became 'all things to all men' (I Cor. 9.22).

This shop-worn phrase calls to mind a frequent misinterpretation of Paul's work among the Gentiles. Was it not for the sake of expediency that Paul carried the gospel to the Gentiles without requiring circumcision? He was a canny organizer and diplomatic administrator who saw that the number of converts could be increased by relaxing the requirements for salvation. Joseph Klausner, the latest writer to defend this thesis, reconstructs the story as follows: Even before his conversion Paul had observed the success of Gentile missionaries who ignored the necessity of circumcision. He had observed that women were easily proselytized because the requirement of circumcision was no hindrance to them. On the road to Damascus, Ananias explained to Paul that the only hope of reaching the Gentiles lay in lessening the burden of ceremonial laws. Why not be satisfied with baptism? In the mind of a practical opportunist, this suggestion bore fruit. It led to concessions which would serve as bait to bring Gentiles into the church. All they should be asked to do was to believe in this Messiah, a relatively simple request (!)[8] To this analysis of Paul's motives some Christian scholars subscribe.[9]

This interpretation is by no means modern; it was the immediate reaction of Paul's Pharisaic brethren when he entered his apostolic career. Well aware of this charge, Paul repudiates it with customary vehemence: 'Am I trying to please men? If I were still pleasing men, I should not be a servant of Christ' (Gal. 1.10). The phrase 'all things to all men' needs to be quoted in its context:

I have become all things to all men, that I might by all means save some. I do it all for the sake of the gospel, that I may share in its blessings (I Cor. 9.22f.).

In this context, it is not a confession of promiscuous tolerance and easy opportunism. It is a mark of complete self-denial, for which Jesus the Messiah and his gospel is responsible. Paul must preach to all men if he is to participate in the good news of a Messiah who, in dying for sinners, abolished all distinctions among them.

There is no distinction between Jew and Greek; the same Lord is Lord of all, and bestows his riches upon all who call upon him (Rom. 10.12).

It is because the Messiah had become all things to all men that Paul must run his race with the same intention.

To be sure, Paul did preach an easier gospel. That's why it was *good news*. It did relax the requirements of moral and ceremonial purification. God in Christ did give men a perfect freedom, in which 'all things are lawful' (I Cor. 6.12). The living Messiah invites all sinners with the call: 'Come to me, all who labour and are heavy-laden and I will give you rest (Matt. 11.28).

But the Messiah who says 'Come' is the Christ of the cross. And his demand is absolute: 'If any man would come after me, let him deny himself and take up his cross and follow me' (Mark 8.34). One hardly comes to such a Messiah by applying tests of practical expediency. When Paul became a disciple, the cross forced him to renounce everything, to count himself as nothing, to share the ignominy and ostracism of his Master. This was harder for him than all his earlier exertions as a Pharisee. And his mission to the Gentiles involved him in unceasing hardship and suffering.

When he proclaimed the word to Gentiles he did not seek to attract by persuasive words of wisdom, by offers of easy salvation. Holding aloft the cross, he made it clear that faith involved a continuing and ever-repeated renunciation of the world. His mission as a Pharisee had been to inflict suffering; as an apostle it was to endure suffering, and to invite others to share that suffering. For this was his vocation as a watchman on the wall, and the vocation of every participant in the mind of Christ.

But his vocation was not merely sufficient to enable him to endure more suffering; it provided a dynamic that generated joy and peace in the midst of suffering. And that is the greater miracle. Although often in prison, he needed no comfort, for he had long since renounced everything but the desire to serve Christ. Though he had nothing, yet he possessed everything. With all human evidence against him, he was utterly confident of the reality of God's power. No weakness of his own could do more than magnify the sustaining grace (II Cor. 6.3–10). No personal misfortune could do more than deepen his trust in God. To be sure, as a Pharisee he had had motivation strong enough to make sacrifices. But he had not sacrificed himself. He had renounced many things, but not the merit of his renunciation. Each sacrifice had been an enhancement of self, an added weight of self-justification, an extra stone in the wall of division. But in the cross, he had been crucified to the world, and the world had been crucified to him. He no longer lived as Paul, but Christ lived in him and empowered him as a suffering servant of the cross. His sufferings were now the true marks of an apostle, because they were the marks of the Lord Jesus. And because he shared the tragedy of the cross, he shared also in Christ's triumph over tragedy, his joy that overcomes the world. Both suffering and joy he welcomed as God's gift in Christ. 'As we share abundantly in Christ's sufferings, so through Christ we share abundantly in comfort too' (II Cor. 1.5).

Paul was a watchman. His vocation was to stand at the end of the age and point to the Messiah's death – and to share that death in joy. His dynamic in a word was the δύναμις of God in Christ in Paul.

NOTES

[1] This essay is drawn from the Hyde Lecture given at Andover Newton Theological School in 1943 and published in the School Bulletin, 36 (1944), pp. 1–11.

[2] H. J. Cadbury, *The Peril of Modernizing Jesus*, New York and London, 1937.

[3] G. F. Moore, *Judaism*, Cambridge, 1927–30, I, p. 333.

[4] *Ibid.*, p 345; cf. Gal. 5.3.

[5] K. Barth, *The Epistle to the Romans*, London, 1933, p. 100.

[6] *Ibid.*, p. 101.

[7] Paul Ramsey, 'The Manger, the Cross and the Resurrection', *Christianity and Crisis*, April 19, 1943.

[8] J. Klausner, *From Jesus to Paul*, New York, 1943; London, 1944, pp. 331–336.

[9] M. Andrews, 'The Conversion of Paul', *Journal of Bible and Religion* 9 (1941), p. 150.

GRATITUDE AND MISSION IN THE EPISTLE TO THE ROMANS[1]

ONE aim of missiology is a more adequate understanding of the apostolic task of the church. One aim of exegetical theology is a more adequate understanding of the mind of a biblical writer. When, therefore, the exegete deals with the apostle Paul, and when missiology accepts Paul's apostolic work as normative for the continuing mission of the church, then these two aims coalesce. This coalescence reaches its maximum when we seek to expound the Epistle to the Romans, for here the mind of the apostle with reference to his own mission is most clearly disclosed. It may therefore be of value to both missiology and exegetical theology if we select for scrutiny several passages in which the apostle indicate a strong connection between his sense of obligation and gratitude on the one hand, and his motivation as an apostle, on the other. The process of selection may be quite simple. We will choose passages in which the words for obligation ($ὀφείλειν$, $ὀφειλέτης$) and for thanksgiving ($εὐχαριστεῖν$, $εὐχαριστία$) appear in contexts significant for our purpose. Romans 1.14 is an example. 'I am under obligation both to Greeks and to barbarians, both to the wise and to the foolish' (RSV. Other translations: 'I am a debtor.'). It was because of this obligation that Paul was eager to preach the gospel in Rome.

The verse under discussion is quite central to the whole passage 1.8–17. We do not follow the movement of Paul's mind until we grasp the inner logic which binds the successive sentences together. And this logic focuses on Paul's sense of obligation, expressed so vividly in v. 14. A failure of comprehension here destroys the full understanding of other strategic verses, including 16 and 17. Furthermore, if we do not get in step with Paul's thought in the introduction to the epistle, the interpretation of subsequent chapters will suffer.

Some commentators, to be sure, minimize the importance of v. 14 by passing over it very lightly. For instance, neither H. Lietzmann[2] nor C. K. Barrett[3] devotes to it more than a sentence or two. The latter writes (in full accord with the former): 'The notion of debt is not emphasized; it is a duty Paul owes, and it is this duty which leads him to Rome.' If such comments are correct, our problem evaporates. Paul was not genuinely in debt to barbarians and we need not ask how the debt was incurred.

Other commentators are impelled by the verse to describe the origin and power of Paul's sense of responsibility for Greeks and barbarians. 'Jesus Christ, the gospel, and his own apostolic office, all lay this duty upon him. . . . Paul knows that he has a responsibility for all, be they Greeks or barbarians.'[4] We may agree fully, and yet suggest that a sense of duty and of responsibility for men may be distinguished from a sense of indebtedness to them. In v. 14 Paul explicitly affirms that he is a debtor to them. We turn, then, to commentators who seek the meaning of this indebtedness.

Of ὀφειλέτης F. J. Leenhardt writes: 'The terms in which he speaks of this [debt] are very emphatic: the grace of God, which has made of him what he is, imposes on him as it were an obligation which he must fulfill by working in his apostolic ministry I Cor. 15.10). None should be cheated of a spiritual treasure which is meant for them; Paul owes it to them and it is incumbent on him to deliver it.'[5] Or again, in a somewhat different view, O. Michel writes: 'Paul is placed under obligation to all peoples and all levels of culture. ὀφειλέτης εἶναι is an image from the laws concerning debts and expresses the fact that Paul himself was declared debtor. The turn of phrase is very strong and says that Paul knew that he was indebted in his whole existence to the Gentiles.'[6]

Even in these comments, however, we discern a continuing difficulty, due, I believe, to the normal conception of debts. In ordinary speech, a sense of debt presupposes (1) a gift from one person to another, and (2) knowledge and appreciation of both the gift and the giver. In this case, it is clear that neither did Paul know his creditors nor had they given him anything. All commentators are surely right in tracing the source of the gift to Jesus Christ, and in stressing the fact that it was this gift which produced in Paul a compelling sense of apostolic responsibility for the Gentiles. The question remains whether we can press beyond this sense of responsibility *for* the Gentiles to the sense of indebtedness *to* them.

A. Schlatter offers a clue when he suggests that the principle which Jesus had made binding on his disciples had become binding on Paul – that his purpose in giving a gift to one disciple was that he might give it to another. This is why Paul was indebted to all.[7] If Paul knew and accepted this principle, then we can understand why a debt to Christ was immediately transmuted into a debt to those whom Christ wished to bring to salvation through them. And who can doubt that this principle was in fact central to Paul's thought? Obligation to him who died produces obligation to those for whom he died. This very 'law' applies with special force to the particularity of Paul's call as an apostle. God's intention in bringing Paul to faith in Christ had been to send him as a 'minister of Christ Jesus to the Gentiles' (15.16). To the extent that Paul was indebted to God for this call, to that very extent he was indebted to those Gentiles for whose sake God had called him. And the same logic applies to every person who is called to any form of διακονία. He is placed under a vast obligation to those whom God intends, through that διακονία, to draw within the realm of grace. Thus faith in Christ inevitably creates a mutuality of indebtedness. It impels the faithful, in love for others, to seek to elicit and to strengthen faith in them. Only faith of this quality is apostolic. Such faith recognizes that the believer is as deeply indebted to unbelievers as to Christ, as deeply indebted to the foolish as to the wise. Here is a debt of whose genuineness there can be no doubt. Yet this debt depends not in the least upon the tangible contributions of the creditors to the debtors, but wholly upon the gift of God in Christ. The character of this debt is indicated by the method of payment: constant, intercessory prayer (v. 9), the mutual encouragement of each other's faith (v. 12), the reaping of 'some harvest' (v. 13), the preaching of the gospel (v. 15). If one is indebted to men because of Christ's grace, then one honours the debt in ways such as these.

It may be said, then, that as Paul sees it, Christ makes every man a debtor to all those for whom Christ died.[8] He thereby creates a fabric of mutual interdependence which defies the usual method of computing obligations in proportion to tangible, direct contributions. This new interdependence is not two-sided but triangular. For example, Paul teaches that Gentiles are indebted to the Jew because Christ became a servant to the circumcised for the sake of the Gentiles (15.7–12). So, too, Paul magnifies his ministry to the

Gentiles for the sake of the Jews (11.13f.). This triangular logic also lies back of his injunction to the 'strong in faith' (who were predominantly Gentile) that they should honour their obligation to the 'weak in faith' (who were predominantly Jewish, 14.1ff.). This obligation was incurred when Christ chose not to please himself but to accept as his own the reproaches which in all justice should fall on others (15.1–3). In Christ, therefore, each man becomes a debtor to every man. This is relevant to Paul's conviction that Gentile Christians owed a debt to 'the poor among the saints in Jerusalem' (15.27). It is altogether too simple to explain this debt, as is usually done, by *quid pro quo* reasoning. Such reasoning can be expressed thus: 'Gentile Christians owed the Jerusalem church for the initial gift of the gospel. They should seek to repay this spiritual debt with material support.' Such an explanation assumes too much. Had these 'poor saints' really been instrumental in evangelizing believers in Macedonia and Achaea? Had they been the ones to commission Paul and to support his campaigns? Nothing of this sort is necessary to Paul's thought. What is necessary is the reality of mutual indebtedness to Christ which is expressed in II Cor. 8.5. Christ had become a servant of the circumcised in order that Gentiles might 'rejoice with his people' (Rom. 15.10). The same grace which had obligated Paul to the barbarians and the foolish had made the 'strong in faith' debtors to the weak whom they despised (14.1–4), and had made all Gentile believers debtors to the saints in Jerusalem (15.27). This common debt gives to believers a common mission, whether the debt be honoured by welcoming all to table-fellowship, by sharing in a philanthropic contribution, or by supporting the missionary campaign to Spain. Those who belong to Christ are debtors whose every act of obedience is an expression of an obligation which simultaneously includes the Lord and those whom the Lord has welcomed.

This understanding of debt underlies the use of ὀφειλέτης in Rom. 8.12. Here, to be sure, only one line of an antithetical couplet appears: 'We are debtors, not to the flesh.' But the context almost shouts the second line: 'We are debtors to the Spirit.' The spirit of Christ dwells in the believer, sealing him as a possession of Christ. This Spirit is alive and life-giving, being in fact the Spirit of him who raised Jesus from the dead (8.9–11). As debtors to this Spirit, men walk by it, putting to death the deeds of the body and suffering with Christ. The debt determines the whole mode of living and

working. When one walks according to the flesh, his existence is
an embodiment of a debt to the flesh (8.12. Gal. 5.3f. gives a parallel discussion of debt to the Law). But if the ultimate debt is to the
Spirit, the whole direction and content of existence are transformed. The whole of Rom. 8 may be construed as a description
of the magnitude of our debt to 'the Spirit of life in Christ Jesus'.
So certain of this is Paul that he detects at once the ultimate form
of apostasy as inherent in any doctrine or practice which implies
that God could or should be indebted to us (4.4; 11.35). Paul's
concept of debt, therefore, has tremendous relevance to the character of missionary obligation: a negative relevance in disclosing the
form of false motives, a positive relevance in accenting the power
of the true motive.

One further observation should be made about this concept of
debt. To Paul the acknowledgement of indebtedness is immediately translated into the sense of gratitude. This is not so for many
people or for many debts. We often respond with repugnance to
the image of ourselves as debtors, just as we instinctively dislike
the image of ourselves as slaves. Most debts represent a burden of
obligation which inhibits our independence. These exert a psychic
constraint which makes us more grateful when a debt has been
repaid than when it was first extended. Yes, in human terms, indebtedness often diminishes gratitude. But the debt of which Paul
speaks is very different. In this case, recognition of debt is synony-
mous with giving thanks. As we turn to his conception of thanksgiving (εὐχαριστία), therefore, we remain in the same circle of
relationships.

The Epistle to the Romans appears to say little about thanksgiving, much less than do Paul's other letters. And in the two
passages with which we deal, the presence of εὐχαριστεῖν is often
overlooked. Attention centres on other concepts, perhaps because
we assume that anyone can readily grasp what Paul means by
giving thanks. A closer study, however, reveals both how central
and how subtle Paul's thought is.

Let us look, for example, at Rom. 1.18–24. What does the
apostle see as the deepest, most stubborn root of sin, the root from
which all sinning springs? What leaves men without excuse? How
do we all become 'fools with darkened minds'? What is it which
brings God's wrath against all the ungodliness of men? Why does
God give them over to the lusts of their hearts? How do men

suppress the truth? The answer to all these questions is the same. And until we understand that answer, it appears to be both anti-climactic and inadequate: 'They did not honour him as God or give thanks to him' (1.21; cf. 14.6). It is usual for men to associate ingratitude with a breach of courtesy or simply a lack of good taste. By contrast Paul associates it with its worst fruits, and by implication views it as worse than all those fruits.

This passage, however, does more than accent the dire results of ingratitude. It makes giving thanks to God virtually equivalent to honouring God as God. To give thanks is to glorify God and to do all things to his glory (I Cor. 10.30f.). This presupposes that all things come from God and are intended to move towards him. It is because men are indebted to God for all things that they should give thanks at all times and for everything. This is the abiding will of God (cf. I Thess. 5.18; Col. 3.17; Eph. 5.20). These are the basic assumptions lying behind Paul's words, but their basic thrust is to make clear the fateful and inevitable results of thanklessness: futile thinking, deceived minds, diseased relationships, enslavement to self, and the resulting malice and covetousness.[9]

It is in another passage (14.1ff.) that we find intimations of the positive power of gratitude. Here again the modern reader easily misses the radical implications, probably because for modern Gentile Christianity the dietary commands of the Torah have lost their crucial significance. In Paul's day observance of those commands had long been regarded as a clear mark of the people of God. It was then a very controversial thing to contend that the act of giving thanks for food had the power to make all foods clean. To Paul this act exerted an even greater power: it destroyed the barrier between Jews and Gentiles, a barrier which otherwise would be insuperable. One man gives thanks and eats: his brother gives thanks and refrains from eating. Their common act of giving thanks not only took precedence over their diverse behaviour; it also established a covenant fellowship which transcended deeply-imbedded and scripturally-supported walls of division, social, economic and religious. The key question becomes not 'Shall I defy the Torah by eating proscribed foods or by treating all days alike?' but simply 'Do I give thanks to God for this food or this day?'. Here Paul had in mind much more than the routine verbal use of a table grace; he was speaking of a pervasive attitude towards every day and everything which that day contains. To give thanks is 'to live to the Lord', accepting from his hand all food and all circumstances. The question of whether we are thankful takes decisive precedence even over the question of whether we live or die. The ground of Christian gratitude is the fact that 'we are the Lord's'. Whatever we do, it is he who remains the Lord, and whether or not we acknowledge his possession of us by giving thanks, the fact remains that all things do come from him (cf. I Cor. 3.21–23).[10]

Viewed in these terms gratitude is inseparable from faith. In the light of 1.21 and of ch. 14, we could emend 14.23 to read: 'Whatever does not proceed from gratitude is sin.' Like faith, gratitude is genuine only as a relation 'between yourself and God' (v. 22). It is genuine only if everyone is 'fully convinced in his own mind' (v. 5). It respects the fact that God has welcomed men whom we feel bound, even on religious grounds, to despise (v. 3). It is wholly contradicted by any action which causes 'the ruin of one for whom Christ died' (v. 15). Thus can all Christian duties be subsumed under the demand to honour God as God by giving thanks. The unity of the church can be seen as embodied in the activity of glorifying God with one voice (15.6). And the mission of the church can be described as the method by which men participate in the multiplication of thanksgiving to the glory of God (II Cor. 4.15), through enabling others to 'glorify God for his mercy' (15.9).

Thus far we have limited our exposition chiefly to Romans. Veteran students of the epistles will be aware that greater use of εὐχαριστεῖν is made in other letters, and that these other letters support and enlarge the argument we have advanced. In I Thess. 5.12–22 the giving of thanks is shown to penetrate the widest range of Christian duties. In Phil. 4.4–7 it is basic to the joy, confidence and peace which belong to those who are 'in the Lord'. In I Cor. 10.23–11.1 it is the link between liberty and love, which enables the apostle to affirm, without contradiction, that his liberty can never be determined by another man's scruples and that he tries to please all men in everything. In II Cor. 4, thanksgiving is both the source and the result of the process of 'being given up to death for Jesus' sake so that the life of Jesus may be manifested'. In Col. thanksgiving is a pervasive motif which gives to the whole letter a distinctive tone, whether Paul is discussing the gospel, the church, its liturgy or its expectancy (1.11f.; 2.7; 3.15-17; 4.2-5).

But we must return to Romans and bring our discussion to a close by reiterating two observations. In the first place, the apostle's sense of debt and his sense of gratitude are not only perfectly compatible but virtually identical. It is not an accident that his assertion of indebtedness to Greeks and barbarians comes within his opening *thanksgiving* (1.8-17). Nor is it a coincidence that his treatment of bitter controversy in ch. 14 should bring into conjunction the activity of thanksgiving and the actuality of mutual indebtedness. In both passages the grateful acknowledgment of debt to Christ is channelled through the honouring of the debt to the wise and the foolish, the weak and the strong. In the second place, it is clear that, to Paul, one's status as a debtor is immediately and totally translated into missionary motivation. The mode and motive of giving thanks can be nothing else but a participation in Christ's ministry to the world. And Christ gave to this ministry such a form that indebtedness to him can be honoured only by indebtedness to those who do not as yet give thanks to God. As an apostle Paul may have received obligations which could be fulfilled only through his uniquely apostolic work and not by all believers. If so, he was charged as an apostle with persuading all disciples to recognize their own obligation to extend grace 'to more and more people' (II Cor. 4.15). His debt was no greater than theirs. Their obligation to serve Christ by serving others was no less inclusive, nor less demanding, than his. *Missionary* motivation, consequently, is not intrinsically different from the motivation expected of all slaves of Christ. Nor can the missionary task be segregated and assigned to a selected few within the church. If there is a difference between the church and the world, it is a difference between those who do and those who do not honour God as God, and this very difference should make those who do give thanks recognize that they are deeply and permanently in debt to the others. And if men are converted from one side of the line to the other, the change will be most authentically indicated by the emergence of a radically new indebtedness/thankfulness. For we, too, are debtors 'both to Greeks and barbarians, both to the wise and the foolish'. Were our gratitude to God to take the form of recognizing our debt to the world, we would have to draw afresh the line between church and world. And with every shift in that line would come a revision in all our thinking concerning what the mission is all about.

NOTES

[1] This essay first appeared in the Festschrift for Professor Walter Freytag: J. Hermelink & H. J. Margull (eds.), *Basileia*, Stuttgart, 1959, pp. 42–8.

[2] H. Leitzmann, *An Die Römer*, Tübingen, 1933, p. 29.

[3] C. K. Barrett, *op. cit.*, p. 26.

[4] A. Nygren, *op. cit.*, pp. 62f.

[5] F. J. Leenhardt, *op. cit.*, p. 45.

[6] O. Michel, *op. cit.*, p. 41.

[7] A. Schlatter, *Gottes Gerechtigkeit*, Stuttgart, 1952, p. 31.

[8] This paragraph is directly related to my interpretation of Paul's aims in chs. 9–11 and 14, 15. Cf. above pp. 17–20, 77–81.

[9] The argument here should be related to that above, pp. 48–51. There we indicated that it was the reality of ingratitude which placed Jews and Gentiles under the same divine judgment.

[10] If members of Groups One and Two gave thanks to God, that act provided a union stronger than any division as defined by the Law (cf. above pp. 83–5). But members of these Groups denied that truth. The only modern writer who has done justice to the ontological significance of gratitude, so far as I know, is Søren Kierkegaard (cf. my essay 'Thanksgiving as a Synthesis of the Temporal and the Eternal' in H. A. Johnson, *A Kierkegaard Critique*, New York and London, 1962, pp. 297–308).

INDEX OF AUTHORS

INDEX OF SCRIPTURE